Emotional Intelligence

A Guide to Boosting Your EQ and Improving Social Skills, Self-Awareness, Leadership Skills, Relationships, Charisma, Self-Discipline, and Learning NLP + Anger Management

© **Copyright 2018**

All Rights Reserved. No part of this book may be reproduced in any form without permission in writing from the author. Reviewers may quote brief passages in reviews.

Disclaimer: No part of this publication may be reproduced or transmitted in any form or by any means, mechanical or electronic, including photocopying or recording, or by any information storage and retrieval system, or transmitted by email without permission in writing from the publisher.

While all attempts have been made to verify the information provided in this publication, neither the author nor the publisher assumes any responsibility for errors, omissions or contrary interpretations of the subject matter herein.

This book is for entertainment purposes only. The views expressed are those of the author alone, and should not be taken as expert instruction or commands. The reader is responsible for his or her own actions.

Adherence to all applicable laws and regulations, including international, federal, state and local laws governing professional licensing, business practices, advertising and all other aspects of doing business in the US, Canada, UK or any other jurisdiction is the sole responsibility of the purchaser or reader.

Neither the author nor the publisher assumes any responsibility or liability whatsoever on the behalf of the purchaser or reader of these materials. Any perceived slight of any individual or organization is purely unintentional.

Contents

PART 1: EMOTIONAL INTELLIGENCE 1

INTRODUCTION 1

CHAPTER 1: EMOTIONAL INTELLIGENCE EXPLAINED 2

    THE CHARACTERISTICS OF EMOTIONAL INTELLIGENCE 2

        Your Self-Awareness 3

        Your Self-Regulation 4

        Your Empathy 5

        Your Social Skills 5

        Your Motivation 5

    WHY IS EMOTIONAL INTELLIGENCE MORE IMPORTANT THAN IQ? 6

    WHAT IS THE COST OF BEING EMOTIONALLY ILLITERATE? 7

CHAPTER 2: HOW TO INCREASE YOUR EMOTIONAL INTELLIGENCE 9

    SELF-AWARENESS TIPS, TACTICS, AND STRATEGIES 10

    HOW TO OBSERVE AND EXPRESS YOUR EMOTIONS 12

    HOW TO EXAMINE YOUR THOUGHTS 13

    INTERNAL CONFLICTS AND TROUBLESHOOTING TECHNIQUE 14

CHAPTER 3: SELF-MANAGEMENT TIPS, TACTICS, AND STRATEGIES 16

    HOW TO RELEASE NEGATIVE EMOTIONS AND EMPOWER POSITIVE ONES 16

    HOW TO FORGIVE YOURSELF AND FORGIVE OTHERS 19

    HOW TO FREE YOURSELF FROM OTHER PEOPLE'S OPINIONS AND JUDGMENT 20

CHAPTER 4: WHAT ARE SUBMODALITIES? 22
Your Critical Submodalities Are What Make a Difference 23
Start Overcoming Your Stress 24
Defining Stress 25
How to Use Submodalities to Get Rid of Stress 26
Being Around Positive People Is Good for Your Submodalities 27

CHAPTER 5: SEVEN THINGS YOU NEED TO STOP DOING TO YOURSELF RIGHT NOW 28
Seven Things You Need to Stop Doing to Yourself 29
#1 - Stop Being Critical 29
#2 - Stop Focusing on the Negative 29
#3 - Stop Reacting 30
#4 - Stop Blaming Others 31
#5 - Stop Looking for Instant Gratification 31
#6 - Focusing on Weaknesses Instead of Strengths 31
#7 - Stop Getting Easily Distracted 32

CHAPTER 6: RELATIONSHIP TIPS, TACTICS, AND STRATEGIES 34
How to Reframe Your Mind 35
Strategies to Improve Your Relationships 35
Managing Other People's Emotions 38

CHAPTER 7: RAISING THE BAR OF YOUR SOCIAL GAME 40
Why Social Skills Matter in Everyday Life 41
How to Improve Your Social Skills 42
How to Increase Your Charisma 44

CHAPTER 8: EMPATH EMPOWERMENT 47
Why Empathy Is Important 48
How to Become an Empath 48
How to Be More Self-Disciplined When It Comes to Your Emotions 50
Five Signs That It's Time to Change Your Mindset 51
Let Self-Discipline Be Your Driving Force 51

CHAPTER 9: LEADERSHIP AND EMOTIONAL INTELLIGENCE 54
The Characteristics of Someone with High EQ 54
How to Use Emotional Intelligence to Lead Effectively 56
How Emotional Intelligence Can Increase Your Chances of Success 57

CHAPTER 10: ALL ABOUT NLP 61

UNDERSTANDING NLP 61
WHAT ARE THE BENEFITS OF NLP? 62
NLP AND EMOTIONAL INTELLIGENCE 63
USING NLP TO BUILD EMOTIONAL INTELLIGENCE 63
PRACTICAL EXERCISES TO ENHANCE YOUR EMOTIONAL INTELLIGENCE 64
#1 Dissociation 64
#2 Content Reframing 65
#3 Anchoring 65
#4 Creating Better Rapport 66
#5 Influence and Persuasion 67
CONCLUSION 67

CONCLUSION 68

PART 2: ANGER MANAGEMENT 69

CHAPTER 1: WHAT IS ANGER & WHERE DOES IT COME FROM? 71

WHAT IS ANGER ANYWAY? 71
WHERE DOES IT COME FROM? 72
WHAT CAUSES US TO FEEL ANGRY? 73
HOW DO I KNOW IF I HAVE AN ANGER PROBLEM? 74
COMMON MYTHS ABOUT ANGER 75
IS ANGER AFFECTING YOUR HEALTH? 76

CHAPTER 2: TYPES OF ANGER ISSUES – THE GOOD, THE BAD, AND THE UGLY 78

THE GOOD 80
SO WHEN DOES IT START TO GET BAD AND UGLY? 81
LET'S EVALUATE HOW ANGRY YOU REALLY ARE 82

CHAPTER 3: HOW TO FIND CONTROL – BAD ANGER, LONG-TERM ANGER, AND EXPLOSIVE TEMPERAMENT 85

TIPS TO START LEARNING HOW TO CONTROL BAD, LONG-TERM, AND EXPLOSIVE ANGER 85
MORE STRATEGIES THAT CAN BE USED TO CONTROL YOUR ANGER 87
A FEW OTHER GOOD TIPS TO KEEP IN MIND 90

CHAPTER 4: REEXAMINING ANGRY THOUGHTS – HOW TO HANDLE LONG-TERM ANGER THAT DOESN'T GO AWAY 91

HOW SELF-DISCIPLINE HELPS HANDLE LONG-TERM ANGER 92

How to Manage Long-Term Anger with Emotional Intelligence 94

How to Manage Long-Term Anger with Neuro-Linguistic Programming (NLP) 95

Expressing Your Anger in Healthy Ways with Communication Skills 96

CHAPTER 5: METHODS FOR DEALING WITH ANGER – RELAXATION TECHNIQUES, LETTING GO, AND FORGIVENESS 98

Learning to Relax and Keep Your Cool – Effective Relaxation Techniques to Help You Calm Down 98

Learning to Forgive 100

Other Methods You Can Use to Help You Manage Your Anger 102

CHAPTER 6: THERE MUST BE ANOTHER WAY – HOW TO SOLVE PROBLEMS WITHOUT ANGER 104

You Also Need to Understand Your Anger 106

Now, What are My Options to Resolve Problems Without Anger 107

CHAPTER 7: AVOID & ESCAPE – CATCHING ANGER BEFORE IT HITS AT HOME, WORK AND PUBLIC ARENAS 110

Catching Anger Before It Hits at Home 110

Catching Anger Before It Hits at Work 112

Catching Anger Before It Hits at Public Arenas 114

CHAPTER 8: THREE DEVILS – THE RELATIONSHIP AMONG ANGER, STRESS, AND ANXIETY 116

Distinguishing Stress from the Rest 116

Is this Anxiety? Or am I Just a Stressed-out Person? 119

Possible Causes of Anxiety 119

How Do I Manage My Anxiety? 120

CHAPTER 9: WHEN IT ISN'T YOU – HOW TO DEAL WITH ANGRY PEOPLE 123

How to Deal with Angry People 124

Learning How to Communicate Properly with Angry Individuals 126

CHAPTER 10: TRICKS AND TIPS – HOW TO HANDLE ROAD RAGE, INTIMACY, AND OTHER SPECIFIC ANGER ISSUES 129

General Tips to Better Manage Your Anger 129

Tips to Help You Deal with Road Rage 131

Keeping Anger Out of Your Relationships – Tips to Rebuild that Spark and Reconnect on an Intimate Level Again 132

Thoughts to Free Yourself from Anger 133

CONCLUSION 134

Part 1: Emotional Intelligence

How to Boost Your EQ, Improve Social Skills, Self-Awareness, Leadership Skills, Relationships, Charisma, Self-Discipline, Become an Empath, Learn NLP, and Achieve Success

Introduction

What springs to your mind when you hear the word *intelligence?* An image of someone brilliant? Individuals who excel in fields, such as science, physics, mathematics, robotics, and other complicated subjects that require a high level of intelligence?

Well, perhaps the last thing that you associate the word *intelligence* with (if you do at all) is emotional intelligence.

According to Daniel Goleman, a renowned psychologist and expert on the subject, emotional intelligence is one form of intelligence that is often overlooked. What we don't realize is that our emotions can represent a *different way of thinking*, and they can be valuable tools, which help guide us in the choices and decisions that we make.

Emotions can be very powerful. If unmanaged, they can overwhelm you and have a large impact on your life. An example of what unchecked and uncontrolled emotions look like would be those that you see suffering from conditions like anxiety and depression. These conditions stem from the inability to manage those emotions, and in the end, they overwhelm you and end up controlling you instead. They make everything seem impossible – which is why you find yourself feeling stuck, miserable, and often like your situation is hopeless.

Being aware of your emotions, and more importantly, *what those emotions mean to you,* is what emotional intelligence essentially encompasses. This book will explore what it means to possess this kind of intelligence and why it matters more than IQ does in the general success of life. You will learn the core principles of what forms emotional intelligence, as described by Goleman, as well as how learning to master these principles will forever transform your life.

Chapter 1: Emotional Intelligence Explained

Emotional intelligence is also known as EQ, and it is described as a person's ability to successfully manage and understand not just their own emotions but the emotions of the people around them. Someone who possesses a high EQ is equipped with the skill to constructively respond to challenging situations, feelings, and people – they can recognize these situations for what they are, and they know what to do.

To successfully build positive professional and personal relationships, you will need EQ. To successfully negotiate challenging emotions, you will need EQ. Developing better EQ means that you will be more self-aware and better prepared to handle interactions, which both happen socially. Most importantly, it makes you become a much more empathetic person overall.

The Characteristics of Emotional Intelligence

EQ is an asset that is considered valuable, and is essentially made up of five core components:

- Your level of self-awareness
- Your ability to self-regulate
- Your empathy
- Your social skills
- Your level of motivation

We will explore these five components shortly – but first, let's observe the characteristics that define someone who is emotionally intelligent:

- **They're Always Grateful and Gracious** – They are thankful for what they have, and they always do their best to exhibit an optimistic and positive attitude, no matter what circumstances may be thrown their way. They never look at a situation as a *glass-half-empty* scenario, and they always manage to see the silver lining where others can't.

- **They Are More Balanced** – It is all about work-life balance. That is how people with EQ maintain their happiness. They understand how important it is to take care of yourself, even when you're putting your 100% effort into something that you're doing. They know that doing too much too soon could lead to burning out quickly, and they always take it one step at a time.
- **They Never Back Down from a Challenge** – Where others might be hesitant to step out of their comfort zone in the face of a challenging situation, people with high EQ see challenges as a learning opportunity and a chance to improve themselves even more.
- **They Make Better Leaders** – Because they can understand the people around them, this is why those who possess high EQ are often found in the top management positions. A person who does not have high EQ will not be able to successfully manage themselves – the people that they work with and the challenging situations which may come with conflict. To be a leader, you *must* possess social skills and empathy for those around you, or you will not have much success when it comes to conflict resolution. High EQ individuals continually work at developing their own awareness and emotions so that they can better understand the emotions of others around them and interact appropriately, especially in business.

Your Self-Awareness

If EQ had pillars which were holding it up, this would be its primary one. This is the foundation of where EQ begins, understanding and being aware of your own emotions.

Essentially, our emotions can be split into two categories. The first described the psychological part of our emotions, and this encompasses our beliefs and attitudes which underlie a lot of our emotions. The second part is the physical aspect, which refers to the sensations that your body feels when it is undergoing a certain type of emotion. When you're nervous for example, what you would feel is panic, shortness of breath, anxiety even, or believing that you can't do something, or that you're not good enough. When you're angry, you may feel your heart pounding and your blood pressure rising. These are examples of the physical aspect and how our emotions can affect us in this manner.

Self-awareness is such an important first step towards building better EQ overall because when you don't realize there is a problem, you won't do anything to fix it. When you're not aware of your own emotions, you won't be able to manage them, especially in situations where you need to the most. Whenever you find yourself experiencing a strong emotion, what you should do is take a step back and assess what it is you're feeling. Ask yourself what you're thinking. How is this emotion making you feel physically? Reflecting upon your own emotions is the first step towards developing a better understanding of them.

Observe your emotions objectively. Be honest about what caused you to feel this way. Be honest about how it is making you feel. Then assess if this is influencing the other people around you.

Emotions are a volatile thing, and sometimes if we don't assess them accurately, it could be misleading, and we end up reacting inappropriately. Did you ever have someone tell you that you're blowing things out of proportion? Self-awareness will make you question your feelings before you decide on a responsive action.

Begin developing better self-awareness by asking yourself the following questions:

- What is the emotion that I am feeling?
- Is this emotion making me feel good or bad?
- When did I start noticing I was feeling this way?
- How long have I been feeling this way?
- What caused me to feel this way?
- Are there any other factors which are contributing to the way that I feel?
- What is the best way to respond to these emotions?
- Do I *need* to respond to it? Or should I just wait for the feeling to pass?

An individual who can make the connection between both the *feeling* and the *thinking* parts of their brain are the ones who have successfully achieved high EQ. Having this ability enables them to form a buffer between their emotions and the way that they respond. They do not act impulsively all the time because of this. They minimize instances of when they were victims of responses which occurred in the "heat of the moment". Their emotions don't control them; they control their emotions.

Your Self-Regulation

Once you've successfully developed self-awareness, self-regulation comes next. This is where you begin to learn how to give better responses to situations. The way you react depends on the kind of circumstances you're facing, and there could be different strategies in play to help you regulate your emotions. An example of some of these strategies would include:

- Actively seek out positive experiences to help balance out the negative moments. When you're feeling down, why not watch a comedy? Or listen to music which lifts your spirits?
- Finding other ways to channel your emotions. For example, if you are feeling particularly stressed or tense, you might choose to channel that emotion through outlets like painting, dancing or even exercising to release some of that pent-up energy.
- Actively avoid triggers which might invoke negative emotions. This could be certain types of environments, people or situations. If it brings out a negative emotion, avoid it.
- Actively try to turn your emotions around by doing the exact *opposite* of what you really feel like doing.

These are just some of the strategies which will help you start better regulating your emotions and be well on your way to becoming an emotionally intelligent person.

Your Empathy

This refers to the ability to recognize the emotions in others. How does someone else feel in a situation? How do they respond to someone or something? This is a skill that is going to take you far, especially professionally, because like self-awareness, having empathy is the key to helping you decipher the way someone else feels. This, in turn, will help you decide how *you* should respond and manage the situation. It will help you determine the best approach to use with them.

Having empathy will help you anticipate the needs of another because you recognize the emotions that they are displaying. It helps you develop understanding and enhances your social skills. It is the tool that you need to help you develop good interpersonal skills, and effectively become an agent of change. It helps you become a better leader, communicate better, and even be able to exercise influential power over the people that you need to manage. It is the tool that is going to help you build and nurture meaningful bonds.

Your Social Skills

Having high EQ is vital if you want to improve your social skills. The most important skill that you could possess to help you survive both in your daily life and in your workplace is effective social skills. This skill is what makes you a good communicator. If you live in this world, you need to relate to others around you. Nobody can survive without having their needs met, and to have our needs met, whether we like it or not, requires the help of other individuals.

The foundation of all human relationships is how well you can bond with another person. Emotions get out of control when poor social skills are a factor. Heated arguments arise, fights happen, and sometimes relationships get severed because misunderstood information hurts feelings. Success cannot be achieved if you're not able to convey yourself properly. When people have a hard time understanding you, how will they be able to get along well with you? If you want to be successful at everything you do in life, you need to be able to communicate effectively and confidently.

Social skills matter at the workplace because it is important to maintain positive and amicable relationships with your co-workers. You are going to spend most of your day working together with them, and without the proper social skills on hand, it can be difficult to build and construct productive relationships with the people you work with.

Your Motivation

Motivation is the driving force that keeps you going even in the face of obstacles. It pushes you to take a leap of faith and make that bold move that not many would dare to do. It is one of the reasons you can accomplish the goals you set for yourself. An individual who possesses high levels of EQ knows how to reawaken their motivation every single day. They wake up in the morning with purpose and a positive outlook. They have trained their minds to only look at the good side, to see the opportunity where many only see nothing but obstacles. Staying motivated every day is something that you need to work at; it doesn't just happen. However, it is a necessary exercise if you want to become a more emotionally intelligent person. Find your purpose and stay motivated by:

- **Frequently Reflecting** – Not just on your current circumstance, but also your progress. It's easy to get consumed by everything that is going on around you, which makes it easy to stop and remember the little accomplishments and small victories you made along the way. Challenges can take a lot out of you, and when you forget, it becomes easier to give up. Make time for frequent reflection to improve your motivation continuously. Don't hesitate to congratulate yourself on a job well done.

- **Get Lost in Someone Else's Story** – Nothing fuels your fire more than hearing motivational stories of how other people have reached their pinnacles of success. True success stories resonate better and have a much deeper impact because they are *true*. Someone else has done it. Someone else managed to overcome the odds. If they can, so can you. Surround yourself with these stories, along with motivational and inspirational quotes as your source of inspiration.

- **Know What You Want** – You can't find the motivation and the drive that you need if you don't know what you want. Your motivation comes from you being able to answer the why question. Why did you get started? Why do you want to do this so badly? What is your purpose?

- **Know What You Need to Do** – Having motivation alone is not enough to keep you going. You need to wake up with a purpose, to *know* what you need to do each day to put yourself one step forward. One step closer to your goals.

- **Mind Over Matter** – Our mind is our most powerful tool. It can either drive us to great heights or hold us back from ever living our dreams. Like every other muscle in the body, the mind needs to be exercised. Mental preparation is the key to boosting your motivation levels. Some of the most successful people in the world start their day every morning by mentally preparing themselves for the day ahead. They meditate, use positive affirmations, recite their goals to themselves or even listen to motivational podcasts on their phones or tablets. Mentally prep yourself every morning and be ready to dominate the day your way.

Why Is Emotional Intelligence More Important Than IQ?

Working on developing your EQ is something that is going to benefit you in the long run. Not only does it improve your leadership skills, but it enhances your ability to negotiate, manage disagreements, collaborate effectively and even be an agent of positive change in any setting that you find yourself in. Humans are social creatures, and much of our success is highly dependent on how well we can interact with others, even though we may not give much thought to it.

According to Goleman, EQ is not that much different from IQ. The quality that distinguishes these two traits is that EQ is focused on *how smart* you are in the way that you interact with your own emotions and with other people. It is not merely about interacting with the people around you, but *how effectively* you interact with them that sets you apart from someone with low EQ.

The workplace is the best situation where the importance of EQ over IQ is most apparent. EQ is a trait that many companies will look for in a potential leader first, not the IQ. This is because a leader's primary job would be to *lead* the people around them. They need to inspire others, get their teams working well together in a cohesive and unified manner, and manage conflict when it arises. All of these skills require the leader to gauge the emotions and read people around them.

Having high EQ is what helps leaders distinguish and identify what an employee's strengths and weaknesses are, not IQ. Having high EQ is what will enable leaders to get along well with diverse groups of individuals, not IQ. To possess great social and communication skills to help you excel in business and with the clients, you need high EQ, not IQ.

Although both EQ and IQ are equally important traits and ideally should be used to maximize your strengths, EQ is without a doubt the trait which is much more important to succeed both in life and the workplace. So much of success depends on how well you manage the challenges that you are faced with, and without being aware of your emotions and the emotions of others, without regulating the way that you respond with high EQ, without effective social skills, without the determination and motivation, and empathy, you will always find yourself falling short no matter how hard you may try.

What Is the Cost of Being Emotionally Illiterate?

Now that we know how beneficial having a high EQ can be let's look at the other side of the coin. What does it cost you if you are emotionally illiterate (when you don't have high EQ)? A prime example would be a time when you mishandled a situation, and it ended up costing you a great deal. You regretted the way that you managed things at the time, and if you could turn back the clock, you would have done it so much better. You are more likely to fall into negative behavior patterns when you don't have high EQ guiding the way. Think of what the compounding effect would be if you reacted negatively and poorly in almost every situation you were dealt with. Things will only get worse for you, and you'll become more frustrated and pessimistic with your life because it feels like nothing ever goes right.

You can sometimes see the effects of emotional illiteracy in some individuals. They become withdrawn, anti-social, have numerous social problems, become problematic and more. Some even deal with depression and anxiety because they don't know how to manage their emotions.

In short, emotional illiteracy is going to affect your overall wellbeing. You will find it very hard to achieve the happiness that you want, which is why it is important to start working on developing better EQ right now.

Chapter 2: How to Increase Your Emotional Intelligence

Working on improving your emotional intelligence is one of the best things you will ever do for yourself. The benefits that it brings encompass so many facets of your life – you won't realize how much of a difference EQ makes until you actually do something to improve it. From interacting with people to keeping you physically and mentally healthy, here are some of the benefits of having high emotional intelligence:

- **It Improves Your Relationships** – Relationships are what life is all about. We've got a relationship with our families, friends, colleagues, partners, spouses, and various other people we meet as we journey through life. Some relationships mean everything to us, and obviously, we want to do everything that we can to keep the relationship healthy. Once a relationship has been damaged, it can often be hard to piece back together – sometimes, it can't be fixed at all. This is why EQ matters. It provides you with the knowledge, tools, and skills that you need to foster and nurture these relationships and to keep them healthy and always thriving. EQ helps you relate to the people closest to you as well as the people around you through self-awareness and empathy. It helps you understand how you should react and respond to situations in the best possible manner. It helps you form deeper, more meaningful bonds because you can understand what the people around you may be feeling and see things from their perspective.

- **It Leads to Success** – Motivation is one of the core concepts of emotional intelligence, and this is the factor that is going to lead you towards success. When you've got high EQ, your motivation becomes much stronger and more focused on the things you need to do. This is because you're no longer easily side-tracked or led astray by your emotions – you know just how to manage them whenever you feel like giving up. You will never see an effective leader in any setting throwing a tantrum, yelling, shouting, and simply handling situations with very poor conduct. If they did this, they would no longer find themselves in a leadership position. With high EQ, you have the confidence, determination, and ability to keep persevering despite the obstacles, and this is what it takes to be successful in life.

- **You Become a Better Leader** – We will explore leadership and EQ in more depth later in this book and see what a difference EQ can make. If becoming a leader one day is something you aspire to be as you progress in your career, this is where EQ is going to help you shine. Those with high EQ make better leaders not because they're so much better than you, but because they can *understand people* much better. They know how to assess the strengths and weaknesses of the team they work with, forge stronger bonds, identify how to regulate the emotions of the team, and bring out the best in everyone. They focus on the strengths of their team and inspire others under their leadership.

- **Optimize Your Physical Health** – Keeping fit and healthy is not just for the sake of weight loss (even though that's the reason so many people do it). It is about making yourself a priority and realizing that your health is one of your most valuable commodities. We often don't stop to appreciate and be grateful for our good health until we fall sick and realize just how much we take our health for granted. Physical health in relation to EQ means learning how to manage your stress levels. Stress can have serious impacts on our bodies, affecting our emotional wellbeing and our physical being too. Without high EQ, you would struggle to manage your stress levels, and it then becomes difficult to lead a healthy and well-balanced life.

- **Optimize Your Mental Health** – EQ can do wonders to help you minimize your stress and anxiety levels. When you've got a better handle on your emotions, you'll know how to manage your moods properly. Learning how to self-regulate is a critical skill, as it can mean the difference between managing well despite challenges, or feeling overwhelmed and sinking into depression. EQ gives you a more positive outlook on life, and with self-regulation, it is easier to see the silver lining in any situation. More importantly, it becomes easier for you to control and manage the way that you respond to situations. Where previously you might have shouted at a person because your emotions got the best of you, with high EQ you can take deep breaths and suggest that things be discussed calmly and rationally.

Self-Awareness Tips, Tactics, and Strategies

Self-awareness. That word alone says it all. Tuning into your emotions is how you get started on focusing on what matters again. When your emotions control you, it becomes easy to feel overwhelmed all the time, lose focus and lose touch with yourself. You're focusing on all the wrong things when you're not self-aware, and you often end up choosing to ignore the problem rather than thinking of ways to fix it – because your emotions are getting the best of you and you "feel like you can't cope".

And if you suppress your emotions? Well, that is only going to make things worse. That's not the right approach to go with either. You may think it's working, but it won't work long term because the more than you choose to suppress everything that you're feeling, the more likely you are to lose control when everything comes bursting forth again.

Self-awareness here means that you need to start sharpening your senses and tuning in to the kind of personality you have. It's time to sit and have a good think about your strengths, weaknesses, what motivates you, what your belief systems are, what influences you and more. Especially your emotions. You need to confront your emotions and no longer ignore them – if that is what you have been doing. Before you can hope to one day empathize and understand the people around you, you're going first need to understand yourself. Having self-awareness is the best approach to start changing your mindset and your emotions. This is a critical step which will lead towards driving you to make the necessary changes that will lead towards better emotional intelligence.

To start improving your self-awareness, use the following tactics and strategies:

- **Adopt the Mindfulness Meditation Exercise** – Mindfulness is exactly what the word implies: teaching yourself to be more mindful. By practicing mindfulness, you are expected to train your mind to focus on your thoughts and be aware of what is happening, what you are doing, and basically, do it with conscious effort instead of running on autopilot. Mindfulness meditation is combining the practice of being mindful *while* you meditate, and it is effective because it trains you to focus on the thoughts that are running through your head at that moment and to properly think about it. Mindfulness will train you to be fully aware of your present state, of what you are doing and feeling at this current moment and exactly what you are thinking about. It forces you to take stock of your thoughts, and process them in a way you wouldn't normally do if you weren't paying as much attention.

- **Make a Priorities List** – Think about what you want to get out of this when you're done. When you make a list, write down what matters to you most regarding working to improve your emotions. What action steps would you take when an obstacle hits and throws your emotions into chaos? This goes hand in hand with setting goals for yourself. Each goal should be accompanied by a priority about *what you want to achieve* from that goal. This helps you stay on track whenever you feel yourself starting to lose sight of why you're trying to become more self-aware in the first place. A priorities list helps you regain clarity and focus. It reminds you that *you can do this!*

- **Daily Self-Reflection Is Needed** – Time to establish a new routine, one where you make time for daily self-reflection to take place. Self-reflection is an important step because without it you won't be able to become more self-aware. If you can find the time to do this daily, that would be fantastic. If your schedule is far too busy, making time to reflect several times a week would do just fine. Even something as simple as five to ten minutes a day for reflecting is good enough to start. Having reflection time gives you a clearer picture of how well you have been progressing so far, and what needs improving. It gives you time to analyze how your emotions have been for the day and if you regulate them in the best way. The best way to approach this would be to have a quiet place to think and to record your reflections down in a journal. It makes it easier for you to look back and reflect on past sessions later on when you've written it down.

- **Don't Spend Too Much Time Overthinking** – The more we think about the negative emotions that we have to deal with, the worse it seems to become. Our minds have a way of building things up and blowing them out of proportion if we dwell on the issue long enough because it gets entangled in our web of emotions. Suddenly, something that is doable seems like the most impossible thing in the world. Worrying and overthinking are two factors which have never helped anyone get very far in life, and only serve to weaken your resolve and resilience if you keep feeding into it. To improve your self-regulating abilities, don't overthink it. When you're faced with something challenging, look at the situation objectively and look at the facts. If it isn't a fact, then don't think about it. Don't embellish, don't assume, and don't overanalyze it; just look at it based on facts.

- **Give Yourself a Purpose Everyday** – Get out of bed each morning with a purpose. Tell yourself, *Okay, today, I have to accomplish,* or *Today I will remain mindful of my emotions throughout the day.* Even if the goal or the task at hand may be something small, training yourself to wake up each day with a purpose and the intention to get things done is what helps train you to get into the habit of paying attention to your emotions.

How to Observe and Express Your Emotions

Observing and expressing your emotions in the right way is the mark of someone with emotional intelligence. But *why* is it so important for us to develop this ability to be aware of our emotions, to regulate and express them appropriately? It is because *you want to be in control* now, instead of letting your emotions control you.

Your future, your success, your relationships, and even your happiness depends on how well you can express yourself. Each time that you respond and react badly to a situation or person, it can have damaging effects on the relationship. Some actions could trigger more unpleasant consequences, sever relationships and put an end to friendships. It is time that you are the one that is in charge, and it starts with learning how to observe and express your emotions, which is the next step in the self-awareness process.

- **Make A List of Triggers** – The first stage towards better expressing your emotions is to make a list of triggers which have, in the past, set off your emotions. This is done through the observation part of the process. Write down the list of triggers you can remember (you can add to the list later if needed), and then write down next to each trigger the emotional response that it evoked from you. Next, write down why you reacted the way that you did. Finally, write down how you would react in the future if presented with a similar situation again. This will help you better express your emotions next time.

- **Identify Each Emotion** – Write another list of the emotions that you regularly experience on a daily and weekly basis. Examine how this emotion makes you feel and react. Ask yourself, *Why do I feel this way*? Are there any underlying factors which cause such a reaction? How do you think you could have responded better, and what would you do to help you manage the next time you experience this emotion again? Reflecting upon and unpacking each emotion gives you time to sort through your feelings. The better you understand *why* you reacted the way that you did, the better you understand why that may not have been the best decision.

- **Checking in With Yourself** – Whenever you find yourself focusing too much on your emotions and things are starting to get out of hand, make a conscious effort to stop. Take a couple of deep breaths with your eyes closed, making a conscious effort to breathe in and out deeply. This helps you pause and remind yourself to focus on the present, and it helps you better express your emotions in the right way to the situation you're dealing with. Connecting with yourself on a deeper level is how you begin making the connection between your emotions and reactions. This will be explored further under the chapters which talk about submodalities and NLP.

- **Maintaining Eye Contact** – When you are around other people or in a conversation with someone, maintaining good eye contact keeps you from getting distracted by your own emotions. This helps you regulate the way you are expressing your emotions when you are communicating with them. Maintaining good eye contact when the other person is talking to you helps you better focus on what they're saying and, more importantly, helps you be attuned to their feelings as they're talking to you. It helps you express yourself in the right way to show that you are engaged with what is going on. It helps you hone in and observe the emotions of the current situation.

- **Giving Yourself Space** – It is okay to take a time out and walk away from the situation if your emotions are threatening to get out of control. Sometimes, we all need a little space to clear our heads so we can regain our thoughts and, more importantly, use that space to calm down. Taking those few moments of calm can make all the difference in the world towards better expressing your emotions moving forward.

How to Examine Your Thoughts

While we may not be able to control life and many things that happen to us, there is one thing that you can always control – your thoughts and your reactions. Having this level of control is an advantage to you. It means that, to some extent, you have a degree of influence and control. All you need to do now is learn how to manage that and make it work to your advantage.

- **Question Your Thoughts** – Whenever you start having thoughts which threaten to spiral your emotions out of control, stop and ask yourself why this is happening? What is the root cause of this thought, and is it justifiable to warrant an emotional response?

- **Don't Fight Your Thoughts** – The more you try to resist something, the worse it becomes. Accept your thoughts and acknowledge them, even if they may be negative ones. Say, *Yes, I acknowledge that this is happening right now and it's making me feel....* Acknowledge it, *but don't dwell on it.* That's the difference. The more you reject your thoughts, the harder it will be to learn how to control them in the long run.

- **Practice Meditation** – This age-old practice has lasted as long as time because of how effective it is at opening up your mind, giving you the mental clarity and focus that is needed to see things in a different light. The benefits of meditation are often underestimated but think about this: there's a good reason why it has lasted so long. Meditation teaches you to breathe, slow down, *take control* of your thoughts by being mindful and helps you feel peaceful and calm, so an overly emotional response is less likely.

- **Patience and Baby Steps** – We would all like to toss our negative thoughts out the window and have them be gone just like that. Unfortunately, it is not quite that easy. Learning to examine your thoughts and control them is a process which is going to take time, and setbacks along the way are to be expected. Managing your expectations is going to help minimize the frustration that you feel when working towards this step. Be patient and take baby steps as you work towards your goal of being able to examine your thoughts better. Eventually, with each little success you achieve, your confidence and level of control will grow along with it.

Internal Conflicts and Troubleshooting Technique

Internal conflict is the struggle which happens *within* you. No external factors are involved here, just what is happening inside you. It almost feels like you are battling yourself sometimes. This often happens when we are unable to fully manage our emotions when we are faced with more than one overwhelming emotion.

How do you manage the internal conflicts that happen within so your emotions don't get the best of you? With the best and most effective strategies below.

- **Talking to People You Can Trust** – It makes a world of difference when you know you've got one, two or several people that you can count on when you just need to talk and get things off your chest. When dealing with internal conflict that you're struggling to resolve on your own, talking it out is the best approach. Don't be afraid to ask for help when something seems too overwhelming. Going through a challenge always feels more manageable when you've got someone you can trust to help you through it.

- **Keep a Thought Journal** – Often, our internal conflict, thoughts, and worries can seem magnified, or possibly worse, when they're bottled up inside our minds with no escape outlet. Keeping a feelings journal is useful in this scenario. Whenever you're faced with an internal conflict, pour it all out into your journal.

- **Sleep** – Simple yet effective. Battling internal conflicts can leave you feeling drained and fatigued. Emotions take a lot out of you and use up more energy than they should when not dealt with properly. When we're fatigued, we're unable to focus or think as clearly as we should. Make it a point to get adequate rest every day, so you wake up each morning feeling refreshed and recharged. It makes a huge difference in your outlook and thought process when you're looking at it from a recharged and refreshed perspective.

Chapter 3: Self-Management Tips, Tactics, and Strategies

Learning how to manage yourself is one of the most important things that you could do towards developing emotional intelligence, especially if you are within a leadership position. You know that EQ requires self-awareness and self-regulation, but it also requires *self-management*. In this chapter, you are going to learn *how to manage* yourself and your emotions, become more focused, and always ensure that no matter what situation you're in, the outcome is always acceptable because of the way that you handled it.

The first step of the self-management process? It's learning to empower positive emotions.

How to Release Negative Emotions and Empower Positive Ones

To allow positive emotions to engulf you, you must make room for them in your life. The way that you do that is by clearing out and letting go of the negative emotions that are currently occupying space. Two strong emotions cannot live in the same space. One will overcome the other, and since it is human nature to veer towards the negative, there must be no room in your life for negative emotions.

The journey to positive empowerment begins now. Utilize the following tips every day, and watch your emotions transform from the inside:

- **Just Breathe** – This is all you need to start. Learn to slow yourself down whenever things feel like they might spiral out of control. Learning to take deep, measured breaths (something you will learn to do once you begin meditating) is an effective technique to release stress. Often underestimated and underutilized, repeated deep breathing in and out will help you relax and loosen the accumulated tension in your shoulders. You can physically feel yourself starting to unwind when you are forced to concentrate on nothing but the air that is moving through your body. With each breath, let go of a negative emotion. Think of it like a balloon, and with each breath you take, imagine the emotion floating away and leaving your body forever.

- **Count It Out** – Along with breathing, you should stop and count to 5 each time an emotion feels like it is going to overwhelm you. You can count to 5, 10, 15 or even 20 – any number that is going to calm you down and stop you from reacting impulsively. Release the negative emotions from your body with each count.

- **Find Ways to Manage Your Stress** – Everyone experiences stress. It just feels like a lot to handle when you're unable to properly cope with it because you've never made a conscious effort to do it before. Things are different now that you are actively working on improving your EQ. To do this, start by pinpointing all the triggers that give you stress and then look at what you can do to change that. Make a list (yes, make a list again) of anything that you feel is causing you stress, and work on eliminating those factors one by one. Stress is a negative emotion, and the only way to get rid of it is to tackle the problem from the root cause.

- **Find Other Stress Relieving Outlets** – Go for a walk, join a workout class you enjoy, go for a hike or a bike ride, find another outlet to relieve your stress instead of just letting your emotions boil and bubble underneath the surface as you try to bottle them up. Negative emotions have to go somewhere; why not multitask and release those emotions while simultaneously doing something that makes you feel good and happy (positive emotions)? If you're prone to being emotionally overwhelmed because you're stressed, it's time to start adopting relaxation techniques. Watch a comedy, indulge in your favorite TV shows, meditate or get together with a good friend so you can have a laugh.

- **If You Need Help, Ask** – Working on eliminating all your negative emotions can be a challenging task for anyone to manage. It isn't an easy journey, and along the way, if you need help, don't be afraid to ask. Your commitment right now is to do what it takes to empower yourself, to fill your life with positivity, and asking for help is sometimes a necessary part of the process. Find someone that you would be comfortable talking to, someone you trust enough to rely on for help. Someone who could offer insight. Surround yourself with people who radiate positive energy – that's another good way to do it. The aura that you surround yourself with will eventually rub off on you.

- **Remind Yourself That Bad Times Don't Last Forever** – Stressful moments and sad times will come and go. Negative emotions do not last forever, although they certainly feel like they do. Whenever you find yourself in emotionally negative turmoil, remind yourself that the storm will pass. That you need to be strong. Over time, you will build up a tolerance and become tougher emotionally as you overcome each storm. The stronger and better you become, the more you will be filled with positive emotions as you slowly begin letting go of the negative ones.

- **Positive Affirmations** – Emotional times can be trying and put us through the wringer, and even though they don't last forever, it can be tough to remember that when you're going through it. Positive affirmations can be your best friend in this case. To start filling your life with positive empowerment, pick a couple of affirmations that empower you, and bring these affirmations with you whenever you go. Whenever negativity starts to get the best of you, whip out your affirmations and recite them over and over until your willpower feels strong enough to resist.

- **Learning to Live in The Moment** – Do you hold onto the past? Has not being able to accomplish something in the past stopped you from getting things done now because you can't let it go and your past failures keep infringing on your mind? Well, you need to stop. This is why you find it so difficult to let go of the negative emotions that weigh you down. Emotionally intelligent people do not hold onto the past; they live in the now. They focus on what they do today to shape the future that they want. They never hold onto the past, but they do learn from it and use those lessons as they make improvements for the future.

- **Knowing When to Take Breaks** – You may be ambitious and determined to work hard to improve your EQ, but you are not a robot or a machine that can work continuously without breaking down. People with high EQ are only human after all, and like you, they get tired. Yet, they still manage to get things done. How do they do it? By knowing when to take breaks. Emotionally intelligent people know how important taking occasional breaks are to recharge and refocus their minds. Feeling burned out and fatigued are not emotions which are positively empowering. Taking care of yourself is how you take the right step towards positive empowerment.

- **Don't Let Your Emotions Distract You** – How many times a day have you paused during a task because you got distracted by your emotions? Where negative feelings affect you so badly that you find it difficult to concentrate on the task at hand? Distractions are everywhere, but people with high EQ have mastered the art of regulating it and not letting their emotions distract them. They can completely remove distractions from their mind when there is something more important to focus on. In this case, positive empowerment. Remove all cause for temptation when you need to buckle down and get something done. Focusing on your emotions never does anyone any good – unless they are positive ones that motivate you toward success.

- **Develop a System That Works for You** – The reason you find it difficult to let go of negative emotions is because you haven't quite latched onto a system which works for you.

Or the current system you have for regulating your emotions is not working well. In that case, it is time to think like an emotionally intelligent person and find a regulation system which works. It may take a couple of tries and practices before you find one that is just right.

How to Forgive Yourself and Forgive Others

We've all made mistakes. There is nobody who can go through life claiming they have never made a mistake since the day they were born. You need to learn to forgive yourself first before you can begin forgiving others. Accept your imperfections because you know those can always be improved.

Holding onto your past and repeatedly beating yourself up over it isn't going to change a thing because it has already happened. You're only human, and if you can accept other people for their flaws, you can certainly start accepting yourself too. Forgiving yourself is the simple part of the process; forgiving others is harder to wrap your head around. When someone has hurt us, especially if the hurt runs deep, it can be hard just to let go and let things go back to the way they were. Sometimes even the thought of the incident that happened is enough to bring all those feelings of hurt flooding right back into your mind, even if it is something that happened years ago.

How do you forgive the ones who have hurt you in the past?

- **By Moving On** – We know this is easier said than done, but it is the only way to begin learning to forgive. Realize that holding onto the past is only hurting you, not them. You are the one that is affected by it. Your emotions are the ones being tormented over the thought of it. Remind yourself that no matter how much you think about it, it is never going to change what happened. No amount of dwelling on the past ever will. The best thing for you is just to learn to let go, leave the past behind where it belongs and focus on looking ahead, the way emotionally intelligent people do.

- **Never Go to Bed Angry** – This is one exercise you should start adopting every night from now on. Make it a habit to never go to bed again with a negative emotion. It is simply not worth it. If there is nothing you can do to change it, then let it be. Why torture your emotions anymore over something that is never going to change? It's an unhealthy habit. Before you go to bed each night, do, watch or read something that lifts your spirits and puts you in a happy mood. Before you close your eyes and drift off to sleep, remind yourself of all the things you have to be grateful for.

- **Accepting Responsibility** – When confrontations and conflicts occur, it takes two people to rock the boat. While the other person may have had a bigger part to play in the falling out, you were also partially responsible on some level. Being someone with high EQ means that you need to use self-awareness to assess the situation objectively, to be able to see what mistakes you made and how you could have handled that better. From there, accept responsibility for the part that you played, and realize that both people involved were at fault to a certain degree.

- **Choose to Be Kind Instead** – Do you have the desire to be right all the time? Even if it means jeopardizing a relationship because you stubbornly refuse to let go of the need to be right? This could be one of the reasons why you're finding it hard to forgive. Instead of choosing to be right all the time, choose the emotionally intelligent way. Choose to be kind. Being a kind person is much better than being someone who is "right" all the time.

How to Free Yourself from Other People's Opinions and Judgment

Emotionally intelligent people are happier and more in control because not only do they not let their emotions control them, but they also don't let other people's opinions and judgments control them either. Caring too much about what other people think is how you get your emotions out of control. Have you ever been upset by what someone else said or thought about you? So worked up that it was all you could obsess about for weeks or months? That's what caring too much about someone else's opinion will do to you.

To possess emotional intelligence means that you need to be confident enough to not care so much about what other people think. You need to free yourself from that chain which could hold you in an emotional prison. Ask yourself *why* you care so much about what this person thinks? What significance do they hold in your life? Do they matter enough to you to let it affect you this badly? If they play no major role in your life, why do you let their opinions matter?

The only opinions that you should care about are yours and those from the people who matter the most in your life – like your family and friends. The ones who genuinely care about you will only want what is best for you. They want you to be happy, and they will do everything that they can to be as supportive as possible.

Free yourself from this restrictive and unhealthy behavior by being true to yourself. Be who you are; don't try to be someone that you are not. You are the one that has to live your life. You are the one going through the obstacles, the challenges, the triumphs, and the successes. You are the one that picks yourself up when you fall – not the people who are passing negative judgment upon you. You only get one life to live, and you shouldn't be wasting any of it on comments which don't matter.

When someone else has a negative opinion of you, it is a reflection on them, not you. It is not a personal attack on you, especially if they are not someone of significance in your life. People are always quick to comment on the negative, and this is a trap you must not let yourself fall into. Brush it off, stand up tall and walk away, reminding yourself all the while that their opinion does not matter. Be confident and believe in yourself, and know what you are worth. Treat the negative opinions and the judgment of others like they don't matter. Because they don't. It only matters if you *let it matter*.

Chapter 4: What Are Submodalities?

Have you heard of NLP? Unless you've already been reading up quite a bit on emotional intelligence, the term might be unfamiliar to you. Neuro-Linguistic Programming, NLP for short, refers to the language of the mind. *Neuro* is the brain part of the reference, while language is represented in the word *linguistic*. To put it simply, NLP is about learning the language of your brain (mind). Here is a simple example to illustrate the explanation.

Picture yourself on holiday in a foreign country – in an unfamiliar territory where nobody spoke your language. You couldn't understand them, and they couldn't understand you. What does that feel like? It's frustrating most of the time because you're constantly struggling to make yourself understood.

That short description is basically the relationship that you have with your mind right now, before emotional intelligence. Without understanding the way our mind works, we will never truly be able to forge a connection. Your unconscious mind is a powerful thing, and when you can tap into that power – to harness it to improve your life for the better – there's no telling what kind of success you can accomplish. NLP teaches you how to become in tune with your mind and understand it in a way you never have before. To help you become more emotionally intelligent, we will discuss techniques in Chapter 10.

Now, we will delve into submodalities and what they mean. Submodalities in the NLP context refer to the five senses that we possess. These senses are *olfactory, gustatory, visual, auditory, and kinesthetic*. These senses are responsible for the kind of experiences that we have as part of being human. Whenever you find yourself being overwhelmed by feelings of negativity, it is your submodalities that help you come out of it.

Some examples of submodalities include the following:

- **Audio Submodalities** – Tone, location, soft, loud, direction, fast, slow
- **Visual Submodalities** – Colors, size, location, brightness, associated or disassociated, near, far, black and white.
- **Kinesthetic Submodalities** – Shape, size, intensity, steadiness, vibration, location
- **Gustatory and Olfactory Submodalities** – Fading out, fading in, change in intensity, change in duration

An example to illustrate this point would be the things that you do to cheer yourself up whenever you're feeling down or depressed. Watching a funny movie, doing an activity that you love, eating your favorite food, listening to some upbeat music on your favorite playlist – these things that you do to make yourself feel better are your submodalities coming to the rescue. Much of how NLP works is by relying on these submodalities to help you change the way that you think, rewire your thoughts and emotions, and help you understand how you have the power to change your mindset and thought process by simply gaining a better understanding of how it works.

Your Critical Submodalities Are What Make a Difference

There are two parts to the submodalities we experience. The first part is where the changes you make have either little to no difference in your mind. The second part is the one which makes a big difference, and this part is known as your *critical submodality*. This is the part that you are going to focus on. By tweaking this part of your brain, you can start making active changes that have a big difference, which is reflected in your external environment. For example, instead of constantly wishing things would change, you now need to fine-tune the submodality which is associated with what you're going through to see real change happening. If you were someone who was previously prone to procrastination before, you need to adjust your submodality so that you will now become someone that is driven by motivation.

These critical submodalities are different and unique to each individual. No two people will experience or undergo the same thing, which is why they can vastly differ. Here is an example of critical submodalities at work.

If you were asked to describe your compelling future, what would that look like to you? Start by picking a goal to focus on. Once you've done that, close your eyes and visualize yourself having achieved this goal. Then, take that picture in your head one step further and imagine you're seeing yourself in a movie about your success. The movie is a storyline of your journey towards reaching your goal. Visualize all of this in great detail.

Now, for the second part of the exercise. It's time to play around and tweak your submodalities to the mental movie you just created. Enhance the movie to enlarge it in your mind's eye. Picture the colors as being big, vibrant and colorful. Sharpen the image and see every detail with clarity. Use your audio submodality to tune into the sounds going on in your movie. What do you hear and how loud are the sounds you are experiencing? Picture this in as much detail as possible. Use the submodalities to adjust the audio aspect of your movie by making the sounds louder or softer.

The third part of this exercise is tapping into your kinesthetic submodality. What do you feel when you visualize yourself achieving this goal? Feel every sensation in your mind's eye, from the warmth of the sun's rays to the cool breeze which may be blowing against your skin. Think about the emotions you are experiencing. Joy. Triumph. Jubilation. Imagine all of this like it has already happened; see it and feel it so clearly that you believe it's real.

That's how you are going to use submodalities to help you enhance your emotional intelligence. More exercises will be depicted in Chapter 10 to help you with the process.

Start Overcoming Your Stress

You need to challenge your stress emotions. Instead of giving into the emotion and letting it take control over you, dictating the way that you respond and react, stop for a minute and just breathe. Stress can have adverse effects on our bodies that we don't often give a second thought to. But we must. If you don't, it will continue to dominate and unravel your entire life, and you will never feel like you have full control.

Start challenging your stress by asking yourself the following questions:

- What is the cause of my stress? The *root* cause.
- What is currently happening that is making me stressed
- Why am I letting it affect me this much?
- What can I do about it? How can I use submodalities to my advantage here?
- How else could I approach the situation?
- Am I able to step back and look at the situation that is causing me stress objectively? Or are my emotions too out of control?

The next step is to challenge yourself by asking if there are reasons why you *shouldn't be* this stressed. Start by asking yourself the following questions:

- Am I stressing myself out by trying to predict the future?
- Am I jumping to my own conclusions and ignoring the facts?
- Is what I'm stressed about going to impact my future in a significant way?

- Will this situation or problem I'm dealing with be as important to me a week from now? A month? A year even?

- If not, why am I letting it control my emotions now?

- How many times has the worst-case scenario happened to me? And if it did, was I able to cope?

- Could I be overestimating the likelihood of the worst-case scenario happening and this is causing unnecessary stress? Or do I have facts to support my concerns?

- What evidence do I have to support that this thought is true?

- Is this kind of stress *that* important that I need to be so consumed by it right now?

The reason why many people become consumed and overwhelmed by their emotions, especially when it involves stress, is that they are afraid their worst fears are going to happen. They are worried that everything they imagined going wrong *is* going to go wrong. They are focused on all the possible negatives of the scenario that they fail to think about anything else. The mind is such a powerful thing that the longer we dwell on something, the worse it seems to become. Some people can even dwell on it so much and believe it to be true that it becomes their reality.

What you need to keep in mind here is that no matter what may be causing your stress, there is always another solution on hand or another way of looking at the situation. In this case, using NLP and submodalities to your advantage. When there are tools available to you, why not make full use of them? Emotional intelligence is yours for the taking, and you're already on the right track to getting it done.

Defining Stress

You're familiar enough with the term, but how would you *define* it if you had to? Stress is an emotion that we experience when we are faced with something that we feel we're unable to cope with or don't manage appropriately, or fear, or feel threatened by. When undergoing feelings of stress, the triggers are often caused by several factors which include family, relationships, work, traumatic events and more.

When we are faced with stress, we might find our heart rates elevating, our breaths getting heavier and faster, a sensation of butterflies in our stomach, or a loss of appetite. Stress is part of our body's in-built emergency system. There was once a time when humans had to protect themselves against predators daily, and this emergency system has stayed with us ever since. It is exactly why humans have survived for so long. Even though we have evolved, our stress response remains intact.

Now, the "threats" we deal with may not be animals in the wild anymore, but our bodies still react in the same way when responding to anything that is considered less than a desirable condition.

That is when the stress response kicks in. Stress in excessive amounts can manifest itself physically. The common symptoms include:

- Frequent headaches
- Loss of focus
- Bodily aches and pains
- Weight gain
- Weight loss
- Decrease in appetite
- Increase in appetite
- Chronic fatigue
- Insomnia
- Excessive sleeping
- Mood swings
- Restlessness
- Depression
- Anxiety
- Anger
- Irritability

How to Use Submodalities to Get Rid of Stress

Among the things that you need to work on when it comes to improving your EQ levels is how to manage and minimize your stress levels. Stress is a common factor you have to contend with until you learn to regulate your emotions using EQ. Even then, stressful situations sometimes cannot be avoided, so the best thing to do is learn how to manage them. What you need to do now is set a goal for yourself. Make this your first step. Pinpoint what those goals are. What do you hope to achieve out of this process? Make it your goal to *want* to overcome your stress levels and rely on submodalities to help you do it.

Submodalities are among the NLP techniques which can help you minimize your stress, either indirectly or directly. NLP is about you making the connection with your mind, to understand the way that it works. Using submodalities will help you learn to disassociate yourself from stress. To keep it at bay, you must disconnect yourself from the emotion whenever you are experiencing it. Whenever you're feeling stressed, concentrate on altering your submodalities to better the way that you feel. Listen to your favorite music or go for a walk to change your auditory and visual perception. This is how to begin to remove and disconnect yourself from that emotion.

Disassociation is one of the best submodality tools which you would use to empower yourself and get rid of stress once and for all. Think of it as the secret weapon in your toolkit to overcoming and regulating this emotion to manage it better moving forward. Now that you know submodalities can be used to *change the way that you perceive things*, you need to use them to change your emotions. Where stress makes you feel intense, use submodalities to make it less intense. This is how you disassociate yourself with it. Think of this NLP technique as a broom that is helping you sweep your negative stress emotions far away from you.

If stress was a picture, submodalities are what you would use to make the picture blurry, bit by bit, until all you see is an empty black box. Whenever stress causes thoughts in your mind to run awry, use submodalities to lower the volume of the noisy chatter that is going on until you completely mute it.

Another way of using submodalities to help you eliminate stress and feel empowered is to start doing away with negative talk. The only talk you should be concerned with is positive. Shifting away from that negative dynamic is how you train your mind to eventually begin to adopt a more positive outlook, just the way that high EQ demands. Use submodalities to place your negative self-talk in a mental box that you never want to open again. You could have all the positive self-talk strategies in the world, but if you don't utilize them, it is not going to do you much good. Auditory and visual submodalities will be your best friend in this instance. Write down your positive affirmations and stick them all over your home or your workspace. Put them everywhere that you are going to see them without fail each day. Stick them on your mirror where you can look at them every morning and night, stick them on the desk beside your laptop, put them on your fridge, put them anywhere where they are likely to be staring you right in the face. It's easier to remember when it's all around you and it makes it easier to retrain your brain when the visual is clear as day right in front of your nose.

Being Around Positive People Is Good for Your Submodalities

The best approach to use can sometimes be to encompass all the five submodality senses. Surrounding yourself from every angle with motivating factors is an effective way to minimize your stress. What better way to stay motivated than to surround yourself with motivational people. Make it a point to keep the ones who inspire you, who drive you, who work hard every day, have big dreams and brilliant minds, in your close circle. The more diverse the company that you keep, the higher the chances of your five senses benefiting from all angles. You will learn so much from being around motivational individuals, and being around people whom you can see pouring their passion into their work and life each day will drive you to be motivated to do the same.

Chapter 5: Seven Things You Need to Stop Doing to Yourself Right Now

Becoming emotionally intelligent is going to involve some rewiring concerning the way that you think. When you look at people with high EQ, observe the kind of positive traits that they emit. One of the qualities you will most often find is positive, and this is because they have trained themselves to think this way. They no longer allow themselves to indulge in toxic and unhealthy behavior patterns that threaten to hold them back from success.

To become emotionally intelligent, you cannot carry around bad habits and negative thoughts. Getting rid of toxic people and surrounding yourself with positive, uplifting ones is one thing – but getting rid of your own negative habits is another aspect you need to look at. Conjuring negative and predictive thoughts in your head before something has happened is known as an unhelpful thought. These unhelpful thoughts and habits will continue to hold you back and prevent you from achieving the high EQ that you want – unless you do something about it.

To achieve emotional intelligence, there are seven things that you need to stop doing to yourself right now. Learning to recognize your unhelpful and negative thoughts is the first step to overcoming them. You are the only one who can accomplish this part of the process. No one else will be able to do it for you. Challenge yourself by now flipping the tables. Drop the bad habits, and start turning your life around today.

Seven Things You Need to Stop Doing to Yourself

We need to understand that much of the time when we let our emotions get out of control there is actually no real basis, foundation, and firm foothold to stand on. The mind is a very powerful thing, and we can easily become a prisoner of our own thoughts without even realizing that it is happening until it is too late. It is because you're carrying around, or you've been guilty of falling victim to, the seven bad habits below:

#1 - Stop Being Critical

We've all been guilty of being too critical at some stage or another. However, this needs to stop because, if left unchecked, it can escalate to unhealthy levels. There could be several reasons why you find yourself constantly being critical of yourself and especially of other people. You could be fed up with someone or something – or your criticism could stem from fear, perhaps even jealousy. Maybe it's even anger and frustration. Your reasons might be different from someone else's, but either way, what can be agreed upon here is that this habit needs to stop right now.

Being overly critical of yourself and others around you can have negative implications. People start to view you as someone unpleasant and undesirable to be around. Arguments are started much easier. Situations get blown out of proportion. You could even end up causing friction in your relationships because of this toxic habit. You know you are in danger of being viewed as a toxic individual when you're constantly judgmental, complaining all the time, controlling, demanding, overbearing, manipulative and quick to anger in addition to being critical all the time. These are all habits of individuals with low EQ, thanks to the lack of self-awareness and self-regulation. This is one habit that you must get rid of to move forward.

#2 - Stop Focusing on the Negative

If all you can think about is being negative, you will never get very far in life. Seeing and staying positive daily becomes a challenge for you. Allowing yourself to remain in that negative frame of mind is going to act like an anchor that drags you down, and the more you dwell on it, the further into despair you find yourself sinking. It will be impossible to accomplish emotional intelligence this way.

Being negative could be something you're so used to that you don't even realize it is your default reaction. Some indicators that you are more negative (than you should be) include if you: find it difficult to accept compliments, always make excuses, react instead of responding appropriately, and constantly find yourself making negative inferences. If you're doing any of these too often, you're likely someone with a negative perception and outlook. This toxic habit is nothing but a breeding ground for failure. Time to put a stop to it!

Positive affirmations can be used to replace negative thoughts that dwell within your mind. Come up with your own list of positive affirmations – sayings that make you feel good about yourself each time you say them. Whenever you feel your emotions threatening to get out of control, immediately whip out your list of positive affirmations and start repeating them over and over again until they sink in and you believe them. Affirmations can be as positive and effective as you want them to be. To see success with these affirmations, you need to make a dedicated effort towards practicing them consistently no matter what. Believing in them right off the bat may prove to be a bit of a struggle, but eventually, it will get easier as it goes on. Affirmations are the key to switching and flipping your mind around, and they need to be a part of your daily routine if you want to experience real change in your life.

Here are some examples of positive affirmations to help you get started:

- My challenges make me a stronger person
- I am focusing only on good thoughts from now on
- I am connected, and I am comfortable with people
- I am in control of my thoughts, and I choose to be positive
- I am more than capable of remaining calm and collected
- I am confident enough to overcome all my problems because I believe in myself
- I am grateful for everything I have in my life

#3 - Stop Reacting

If you react more than you respond, then you know what to do... STOP. If you continue letting your emotions be in the driver seat, you will never be the one in control. You will always find yourself making a bad judgment and poor choices, reacting very poorly to any situation that you are in. This will only reflect negatively upon you, and show everyone else the kind of character you possess. If you don't want to be viewed in a negative light, you need to stop reacting instead of responding.

Those who are often driven by their emotions react more than they respond because they lack self-awareness and self-regulation. They don't stop to think about the consequences of their actions. They don't worry about the repercussions, and they don't realize that sometimes saying sorry may be a case of too little too late. Being able to say sorry does not give you the freedom to behave any way you like. Nobody will be willing to put up with that kind of behavior for long. Emotional intelligence defines and determines how successful a person you are going to be and what kind of leader you could make. A person who reacts rather than responds will never be a good leader.

Meditation, relaxation, and breathing are three very helpful exercises that can help you regulate your emotions and keep you from overreacting. Meditation and relaxation can help you manage your stress levels, while breathing will help keep your emotions in check. Meditation, relaxation, and breathing work because they help make the body physically feel calmer in addition to helping you develop emotional and mental calmness as well.

#4 - Stop Blaming Others

Another toxic habit that someone with low EQ has is that they constantly see themselves as the "victim". It is always someone else's fault, never theirs. External factors are always to be blamed; it is either a person or a circumstance that caused them to fail. They are unable to see their own flaws, which is why they find comfort in pointing the finger and blaming someone else's instead.

This toxic behavior just goes to show poor character, and you will never become a leader if you don't drop this habit pronto. It may be easier for you always to blame someone else rather than accept responsibility for your part in the process, but that does not make it right. You know it isn't right, so why keep doing it? Blaming others all the time just makes you an ineffective person, someone who is destined never to reach success because this attitude is going to hold you back.

It takes real courage to own up to your mistakes, take responsibility and be accountable for your actions. This is why emotionally intelligent people fare so much better than those who lack that trait.

#5 - Stop Looking for Instant Gratification

A sign of emotional intelligence is being able to see the bigger picture. Those who don't have high EQ always look for the shortcuts – the easiest way to get it done. They only seek instant gratification, and they are never able to sustain their motivation for long because they tend to give up when things become too challenging. Thinking that instant gratification is better than the long-term sacrifice is where so many people fail. Instant gratification will never amount to long-term success; it is only a distraction and temporary satisfaction. Sooner or later, you will fall back into that old pattern of being dissatisfied with life in general because things are still not what you thought they would be.

This is why motivation is one of the five core concepts of emotional intelligence. It is a reminder that you need to keep going and realize that every step that you take must be one that leads you closer to your goal. Emotionally intelligent people are not bothered by the distractions and the difficulties along the way because they have the bigger picture in mind. They know what they want, and they will not be dissuaded by the temptation of instant gratification. This is the mark of a leader, someone who can keep their eyes on the prize. Someone who can think ahead and see a vision that no one else can see. To become this person, you need to drop the habit of constantly being tempted to go down the path that leads to instant gratification.

#6 - Focusing on Weaknesses Instead of Strengths

It is hard to reach your full potential when all that you keep fixating on is all the things that you are *not* good at. A leader with EQ is not someone who dwells on weaknesses; instead, they focus on their strengths and the strengths of the people around them.

Everyone has weaknesses and things they would like to work on. Even you by picking up this guidebook are acknowledging that improving your EQ is something that you need to do. That is already a good sign of progress, *knowing that something needs to be improved*. The thing about weaknesses is that they can always be fixed if we have the determination and drive to work on getting rid of them.

Stop focusing on your weaknesses and start rewiring your brain to focus on the strengths that you bring to the table. List all the qualities that you are good at. If you're having trouble with this, ask family and friends for feedback. However, you *must* learn to accept the compliments that they give you, and not brush it off or try to downplay it. That's reverting back towards focusing on your weaknesses again. Focusing on your weaknesses is putting limitations and boundaries on yourself. You're creating mental blocks before you have even attempted to begin.

The time has come to start embracing the strengths that you have and start tapping into them to improve your life and your emotional intelligence levels significantly. Also, start practicing gratitude every day. Gratitude is one of the healthiest positive emotions that we can feel as a person. Do you notice how those who are always grateful somehow seem like they are more resilient to stress? Or even if they are going through moments of stress, it rarely ever shows as much as their gratitude does? Not only does gratitude actively remind you of the things you have to be grateful for, but when you actively remind yourself of all the good experiences you have in your life, it eventually helps magnify positive thoughts, and soon, the positive thoughts will be strong enough to overpower the negative and toxic emotions.

#7 - Stop Getting Easily Distracted

Here's the difference between you (in your current state) and an emotionally intelligent person: the latter has managed to achieve the goals they set out to do; you have not. Do you know why? Because you're easily distracted – another toxic habit which you need to stop doing to yourself. While an emotionally intelligent person is focused on seeing their goal through to the end, someone without that same EQ level is easily distracted because they are never satisfied.

Those without EQ are constantly discontent, looking for something bigger and better to come along. They jump from one thing to the next, hoping for faster or more visible results. This approach is never going to work. It is always easier to start something new, but to see it through to the end is another story – which is why you *need* emotional intelligence on the long, hard road to success. Starting something is always new and exciting, but keeping that momentum and motivation going is where you're going to need to rely on your EQ to help you see it through. When you start a new project or a goal, commit to seeing it through to the end, *especially* when the going gets tough. This is where your emotional intelligence will help you get through it the most. Those with high EQ are never quitters, and they never allow themselves to be deterred no matter how hard things may seem.

Sometimes it is hard not to get distracted. Staying focused on a task all the time requires a lot of energy. To help you stay on point: stay focused on your goals, find ways to control your internal distraction (like working in time blocks, for example, while taking short breaks in between), and keep your external distractions to a minimum (put your mobile on silent when you need to focus on a task at hand). Moreover, and most importantly, never forget why you set this goal for yourself in the first place.

Chapter 6: Relationship Tips, Tactics, and Strategies

The relationship that you have with yourself and with others depends on how good your EQ levels are. People with higher EQ have more fruitful, productive, healthy, and happy relationships (this encompasses all types of relationships). It is difficult – sometimes impossible – to cultivate a positive relationship with someone who is emotional all the time. An emotionally unstable person is someone who is difficult and unpleasant to be around. If you wouldn't want to be around someone like this, why would you think anyone else would?

People are unique creatures. Not everyone is going to share the same point of view. What works for you may not necessarily work for someone else. Who would have thought that so much of our world revolves around our emotions and how well we manage them? Most people don't even give much thought to emotional intelligence until it is pointed out to them just how valuable and important this type of intelligence is – especially what a difference it can make to the kind of relationships you foster with others.

To become the emotionally intelligent person you want to be, you're going to have to undergo a process called *reframing your mind*. This means you need to strengthen your EQ by changing the way that you think, particularly in the moments when you are unable to regulate your emotions. Reframing your mind is the thing that is going to help you manage your emotions the way an emotionally intelligent person would. You need to do this first before you begin working on improving your relationships because it simply isn't going to work if you maintain the same way of thinking.

How to Reframe Your Mind

Reframing your point of view is essentially changing your mind – a mind over matter exercise. If you put your mind to it, you can do it. The following exercises will also help with the process:

- **Make Time for Problem Solving** – Part of reframing your mind is to change the way that you think and approach problems. Where previously it might have caused you a lot of stress, and your approach was to feel like you're unable to cope, this now needs to change. The self-regulation part of the EQ process requires that you be able to solve problems. This can be strengthened by setting time aside regularly and analyze the problems you are currently facing or have previously faced. When you sit down to approach the problem, do so with a clear, calm head. Reflect upon the problem, and plan a few action steps of how you would resolve the situation. Reframe your thoughts to see these problems as opportunities to work on improving your EQ instead. Shed a positive spin on it.

- **Step Outside Yourself** – With some practice, you'll be able to eventually "step outside yourself" and observe your actions like you would if you were a third-party observer. Imagine that you were on the outside looking in, looking at the kind of person you are and the way you handle things. Do you like what you see? From an outsider's perspective, how would you say things could be handled better? Where do you think your current emotional intelligence levels are at? Taking time to reflect upon yourself will bring you to a greater level of self-awareness, which is the primary component to begin developing your EQ. Only when you can accept and embrace what is happening and not live in denial can true change start to happen.

- **Stop Making Excuses** – Excuses do nothing for you except to distract and deter from focusing on what's important. They don't do you any good, and it is time that you dropped them. Using excuses to rationalize your decisions and reactions, to explain away behavior which you know deep down is not acceptable, is not the mark of someone with high emotional intelligence. Excuses will always keep you in your comfort zone and prevent you from achieving success. Excuses will prevent you from ever learning how to regulate your emotions and develop empathy. Excuses are not productive.

Strategies to Improve Your Relationships

An important step in improving relationships is about being *present*. This is vital to the survival of any relationship. When you are distracted, you waste a lot of your time on the things which you cannot change instead of focusing on the things that matter right now. You forget the little things you have to be grateful for, the relationships you have with the people who are around you, and completely neglect your present.

When you are distracted and focused on your emotional turmoil instead, you forget that the present is *precisely what you should be focusing* on because it is going to determine and shape what happens to you in the future. The strength of a relationship lies in the precious moments that you spend and build on together, and you can't do this when your mind is elsewhere and not focused on the time that you're given now. Once a moment is gone, it can't ever be brought back, and when life is as fleeting as it is, the last thing you want is to be living with regret.

Maintaining relationships is hard work, and the last thing you want to add onto the already heavy workload is having unregulated emotions added into the mix. By being present, you are in control of two very valuable tools – *self-awareness and empathy.* The two components make up emotional intelligence. When you're attuned to what is happening around you, you're able to respond accordingly. The type of attention, empathy, and awareness is important in a relationship. Relationships are a two-way process, and everyone involved needs to play an active role in the process if it's going to work.

The way that your partner looks, moves, the tone of voice they use and how they react during a conversation with you will tell you much more about what they're truly feeling on the inside instead of what they're saying with their words. This is where empathy and awareness are going to help you out. The person could be saying they're fine, but if you show up, be present and watch the non-verbal cues that are being emanated from them, it'll clue you in to whether they are as fine as they say. Non-verbal communication is just as powerful as verbal communication because even when the person is sitting in silence, they are communicating through their body language – even if they may not be aware of it. If you're not being present, you're going to miss all of this and put your relationship at risk because it would seem as if you don't care enough.

Being present is the key that you need to enhance the potency of the bond you've already forged in your relationship. You don't have to be the most emotionally intelligent person in the world immediately to start building a stronger relationship. All you have to do is show up and be present. When you aren't present, you miss a lot of information, valuable information, which you could have used to strengthen your bond. When you're not fully present in the moment, as much as you think you've done a good job of hiding it, you'd be wrong. All you need to do is notice the next time someone isn't fully present when you're speaking to them. It's noticeable, and it shows, especially when you are the one giving them your undivided attention. If you notice, you can bet your partner will notice it too.

To start improving your relationships, work on the following strategies:

- **Don't Be Afraid to Ask Questions** – Asking questions is how you get to know the other person and build bonds. A connection cannot be made if you don't know anything about the other person. Even if you know the person well, never be afraid to always ask more questions. It shows that you are genuinely interested in them, and more importantly, that you are present and living in the moment.

- **Communicate in an Honest and Open Manner** – It is important to be as honest as possible when communicating with the people around you, even if what you have to say may not be exactly what they want to hear. Emotional intelligence means learning to be comfortable expressing your opinions freely even if it means the other person may disagree with you. Disagreements are not a personal attack on you, and not everyone is going to share the same opinion all the time. You'll feel much better knowing you've given your honest feedback instead of living with a little white lie. Relationships built on lies are not a firm foundation which will stand for long.

- **Keep Your Tone and Language in Check** – When attempting to communicate, you – as the communicator – need to ensure that you frame those messages in a clear, easy to understand language. Dealing with emotions can be tricky because you don't want to come off the wrong way, which is why *the way that you communicate* in the relationship (any relationship) is going to make a lot of difference. Ideally, it should be in a manner that will not risk offending or injuring the feelings of the other person. The language you use should also be concise and to the point. Use self-awareness to assess the situation that you are dealing with, and change your tone or language to match the need of the situation. That is what someone with high EQ would do.

- **Get Some Feedback** – This is how you tell if you are helping with the situation, or making it worse. To ensure that you are being effective in the relationship, you need to constantly seek feedback at every change that you get. Does this person get where you are coming from? Are you connecting the way that you want to? Is there something else which could be done to help strengthen or nurture the relationship? Play out scenarios to your family and friends, act out your reactions and get them to give their honest feedback about how they think you handled the "pretend" situation. This helps you gain a better understanding of how you're doing, and you'll be able to take notes (maybe even helpful tips) about what else you could do to improve moving forward.

- **Pause, Think, Speak** – Emotionally intelligent people are ones who do not blurt out the first thing that pops into their head (because they know that by doing that, you run the risk of saying the wrong thing or causing misunderstanding). Once something has been said out loud, it cannot be unsaid. Self-regulation calls for you to pause and think before you speak. Do not give in to the urge to respond with the first thing that pops into your head; it is completely okay to pause for a moment, take a beat to really think about what you're going to say, and then speak. It will help you avoid much confusion and misunderstandings in the long run, and you end up building a better bond with the person in the process. Or strengthening your existing bond when the two of you have a healthy and happy relationship.

- **Positivity My Friend** – Emotionally intelligent people are always positive. That is part of what makes them so likable, and how they manage themselves and other people so well. Imagine a situation where someone is speaking in a bright, cheery manner with a smile on their face. Now, imagine another person, who is speaking in sullen, somber tones with a serious look or frown on their face. Always smile because a positive attitude does make a difference, and nobody can resist a person who radiates positive energy. Building bonds and strengthening relationships is that much easier when you've always got a smile on your face and an upbeat attitude that makes someone else smile.

Managing Other People's Emotions

Managing other people's emotions effectively requires that you remain calm. This can only be accomplished once you have achieved self-awareness, self-regulation, and empathy. You need to respond without reacting just as emotionally, even though the situation may be challenging on you. The only way you can handle it is if you are aware of your own emotional triggers and have regulating strategies in place to help you control them.

Here are some strategies which you may find useful in helping you manage the emotions of others:

- **Let Go of Your Pride** – Don't let pride or ego get in the way of you being able to manage relationships effectively. These two traits are going to be barriers and prevent you from empathizing the way that an emotionally intelligent person would. If you want to learn how to manage someone else's emotions successfully, you will have to start by tossing ego and pride out the window. Don't let stubbornness get in the way of being able to see the bigger picture. Learn to see things from their point of view, and ask yourself why they are reacting this way and what you can do to make the situation better. This helps you strengthen your empathizing skills and teach you how to handle similar situations in the future. To successfully manage someone else's emotions, you may have to be the bigger person.

- **Don't Judge** – One of the most important steps in learning how to manage others is to listen to them without being judgmental. It may be a challenge, but you need to not let your personal biases or preferences get in the way of the situation. To effectively manage someone else's emotions, you must deal with it with an open mind. Don't come into the situation with preconceived notions of what you think is right or wrong, or how you think they should be. What you think may work for you, but it won't necessarily be the best solution for them.

- **Let Them Have Their Space** – If needed, allow that person to have their space. Sometimes that could be the best thing to do, depending on the situation. Or encourage them to talk to you and let it all out. For example, if the person you are trying to help is crying as part of their emotional response, let them. They may be in need of an outlet to release all that pent-up emotion before they can begin to feel better. If they need some space for a couple of minutes, let them. What you basically need to do in this situation is be the missing support system that they need to feel better. That is how you help them manage their emotions effectively.

- **Identify Their Emotions** – This is where your skills of self-awareness and empathy are going to help you out. When the person you're trying to handle is just one big emotional mess, you need to step in and be the objective one. Observe them and use your empathy skills to begin identifying what emotions they are displaying. Gauge the way that they may be feeling. When you can successfully identify the emotions that you're dealing with, you will be able to think of more effective solutions because you know what you're dealing with.

- **Ask Questions** – The more questions that you ask, the more information you receive. The more information you receive, the better the solution you can come up with. Open-ended questions which encourage the person to talk and reveal more information is the best approach. You need to get a clear picture of what you're dealing with so that you can identify the problem, then plan the appropriate response or solution. Essentially, you need to get that person to reveal their story. There is always a reason why they are emotionally that way, and it is up to you to try and pinpoint what the cause is if they cannot help themselves.

- **Be Okay With Apologies** – If at any point during the course of your interaction you may have done or said something that makes the other person feel worse, be okay with apologizing. When you have to manage someone else's emotions, it is not the time to be too proud to say that you are sorry, even if you believe you are right. You need to keep the peace, be the level-headed one in this situation, and once again be the bigger person. Be ready and willing to sincerely apologize if the situation calls for it.

Chapter 7: Raising the Bar of Your Social Game

By nature, humans are very social creatures. However, since the dawn of technology and the age of smartphones, this quality seems to have fallen by the wayside. It is easy to overlook how important social skills are, but think about how much you rely on them without even realizing it.

You rely on social skills to communicate with friends and family and to communicate with strangers at the store when you run errands to meet your needs. These skills are even more important in the workplace because without social skills it will become nearly impossible for you to climb the career ladder. Observe the leaders in top positions at your job right now. They're likely not individuals who will just keep to themselves, actively avoid others, and not hold a proper conversation when needed.

To thrive at the social game, you need emotional intelligence. When you understand your own emotions, it makes it easier to manage and gauge the emotions of everyone else around you. To be successful at life in general (not just in your career), you will need a combination of both high emotional intelligence and excellent social skills. Emotional intelligence will help you:

- Empathize with others;
- Understand and be able to put yourself in their shoes;
- Interact with a diverse group of people;
- Be influential;
- Be persuasive;
- Form close bonds with others;

- Nurture meaningful relationships; and
- Work well with others in a group or team setting.

Building healthy relationships requires us to be in tune with the emotions of others. This helps us respond and react appropriately. We may think that our social and emotional world are two different components, but in reality, they are more connected than you may think. What kind of feelings do you usually experience in a social setting? Happiness? Love? Anger? Frustration? Guilt? Excitement? Joy? Optimism? Compassion? Satisfaction? These are all social emotions that exist *because* of the relationships we have with the people around us – which means that if you want to build healthy relationships, you need to be in touch with not just your own emotions but theirs too. This is where emotional intelligence comes into play.

Emotions are contagious – yes, just like the flu. A perfect example to illustrate this point would be if you have ever been around someone who just radiated negativity. Notice how your mood dips and how drained of energy you feel just being around that person – almost like your happiness is just ebbing away. Their negativity starts rubbing off on you, and even after they have left, you're still feeling the effects that they left behind. See how emotions can spread just like that? Your mood affects others more than you realize. If someone else's emotions can affect you so strongly, you can be sure your emotions are doing the same thing.

Why Social Skills Matter in Everyday Life

Each day, from the moment you walk out the front door of your home, you are within a social setting. You walk past or greet people on the streets, on public transport, in the supermarkets, at work. Even if you're spending the day running errands, you need to rely on social skills to help you converse with others because you may need their help for something. Like when you're buying milk at the store, you need to thank and greet the cashier. That's a form of social interaction.

As long as you are surrounded by people, you will need social skills to relate to them. Even for basic survival. If you're someone who is ambitious and has high hopes of climbing the corporate ladder of your company one day, social skills matter – especially when your performance depends on how well you can share your ideas and productively contribute to your team and the organization. With high emotional intelligence and social skills, you will be viewed as an asset. No matter how good you may be at your job, you won't get very far if you can't communicate well with the people and the clients that you have to work with. If you want to succeed, you need to become that person who is approachable, amiable, pleasant, and who makes others feel comfortable in their presence.

The good news here is that social skills are something which you can learn and develop. Even if you may have been terrible at it before, don't worry. This is why you're reading this book – to improve and discover what you can do and how emotional intelligence can help you make better conversation from this point forward.

How to Improve Your Social Skills

To start improving your social skills, you need first to do a quick reflection on your current social circle. How do the people around you now make you feel? Since our emotions are often influenced by the people around us and vice versa, this is a necessary step of the process. To become better at the social game, you need to build a better, more positive social circle. There is no way you can maintain emotional intelligence and excellent social skills if you are surrounded by negative people all the time because that is going to make you a more negative person. Someone who is negative does not possess high levels of emotional intelligence.

Part of being emotionally intelligent is surrounding yourself with the right kind of people. Successful individuals do it all the time, and they are constantly advising the rest of us to do the same. If your current social circle is not doing that for you, it might be time to form a new social circle, one filled with those who only bring positive attitudes to the table. This may not always be easy to do because sometimes the negative ones could be people we simply cannot avoid (family, relatives, co-workers). What you can do instead is try to fill your life with more positive people to balance that out.

Wondering how to go about meeting new people? Try any of the following suggestions:

- o Join a new club (something that interests you like a book club, garden club or cooking class)
- o Become a volunteer for a cause you believe in
- o Join the gym (great way to get in some exercise too)
- o Sign up for a new class (dance, Zumba, yoga)
- o Join community activities

You get the idea. When you get the chance to join or try something new, go for it. You never know where it could lead or what connections you could end up making.

Other things you could do to improve your social game include:

- **Be Yourself** – Never be someone you're not. That's just a recipe for disaster. True, you're trying your best to improve your social skills, but you still need to be genuine about it, or you risk coming off as insincere. If you have ever encountered someone you thought was completely insincere, then you will understand exactly *why* you should not repeat that mistake. If you attempt to compliment someone in a social setting, make sure that you are sincere about it, or don't say anything at all. It is better than risking sounding like a phony and putting people off because they got the wrong impression about you. Offering a compliment that you don't mean is still a very risky endeavor because your words may be saying one thing, but your body language is saying something entirely different. Be yourself because you are lovely just as you are, and part of being emotionally intelligent is having the confidence to believe in yourself.

- **Make Remembering Names a Priority** – If you want to make an excellent first impression every time, make it a point to remember the names of the people you're talking to, especially when you're meeting them for the first time. Make eye contact, smile, introduce yourself with a firm handshake, and repeat their name when they say it to help you better remember. When they introduce themselves by saying, *Hi, I'm Jen,* what you need to do is respond, *Hi Jen, it's lovely to meet you, I'm (name).* That way, the next time you engage with them in a social setting, and you can remember who they are, they will instantly warm up to you, and your social skills have already improved just like that. Think about how you've felt when someone remembered your name as opposed to when you've had to re-introduce yourself to someone you've already met previously. Doesn't feel very good, does it?

- **Minding Your Manners** – Sometimes, it is the smallest things which can make the biggest difference in the world. Something as simple as having good manners can go a long way in dramatically improving your social skills. A sign of someone who possesses high emotional intelligence is their ability to remain polite, respectful and well-mannered in every situation, even the ones which are challenging. When someone is being rude to you, but you make it a point not to stoop to their level, this says a lot about who you are as a person. Always make having good manners a priority and your social skills will improve by a mile.

- **Be Present** – Sometimes, it can be easy to get distracted, but if you want to become much better socially, you need to make it a point from now on to be present in every conversation and social interaction that you have. Be *fully* present, attentive and alert. Treat every social interaction the way you would if you were sitting in on a very important client meeting. It deserves that same kind of focus, that 100% attention. If you are interacting with someone, make an effort to minimize the distraction by putting away your mobile phone and do your best to ensure that your mind is not preoccupied at that time. This is a sign of someone with high emotional intelligence, someone who sees the value in meaningful conversations and makes an effort every time. This is the factor that makes all the difference in the world. When you actively listen to what someone else is saying to you, it minimizes the chance of awkward silences and conversations with a taper off because you're unsure what to say or what the appropriate response should be. Mastering social skills means knowing how to keep the conversation bouncing back and forth, processing the information that you receive, and leave anyone you're talking to with a positive impression. This ensures that you are memorable and they can't wait to get in touch with you again.

- **Have a Goal for Yourself** – When you are just starting out at working to improve your social skills, it helps to set little goals for yourself in the beginning. Start with small goals like, *Today, I will make it a point to converse with three people and make it meaningful*, and work from there. Improving your social skills is about practicing until it becomes second nature to you, and what better way to do this than to have daily or weekly goals that push you to keep moving forward.

How to Increase Your Charisma

Social skills and emotional intelligence are just the beginning. If you really, want to give your social skills a boost, there's something else that you need to add into the mix – charisma. Individuals who ooze charisma seem to have this uncanny ability to just draw people into their circle the minute they start talking. They have confidence, and they just seem to charm you with every word they say right from the beginning. That's charisma working its magic.

There are some lucky few out there who have been fortunate enough to be blessed with a natural charismatic ability. For the rest of us? We need to work on developing it. Just like confidence, charisma is something that you need to work on and exercise daily. It is going to take time and practice, so you're going to need to be persistent with it until you get there eventually.

If you're ready to start working on becoming the charismatically cool cat you've always wanted to be, here's how you can get started:

- **It's All About That Smile** – A smile should be genuine, never forced. A smile should reach your eyes, not something that is stiff and giving away how uncomfortable you really feel. Practice smiling in front of the mirror every day until the smile that you see is one that is warm, genuine, friendly, relaxed and natural. That is the smile of someone who has charisma. A genuine smile lights up your face and makes you appear more pleasant, likable, and approachable. You will rarely find someone who won't return a genuine smile. When you smile, you put the people you're interacting with socially in a more relaxed, comfortable and happy state, which will make them gravitate towards you even more – because you make them feel so good. Maintain eye contact when you smile too, don't forget that bit.

- **Eye Contact in the Right Dose** – Too much eye contact and you come off as someone who is creepy and uncomfortable. Too little and you appear aloof and unapproachable. Mastering just the right amount of eye contact is the key to becoming more charismatic. In every social setting, no matter who you may be speaking too, having the right amount of eye contact is very important. Eye contact lets the other person know that they matter and are worthy of your time and attention. Keep eye contact, but not to the point that it seems as though you're staring them down, trying to intimidate them. The best eye contact length to maintain is to hold a person's gaze for one second longer than what you would normally do. Just like smiling, practice this at home in front of a mirror until you are happy with what you see. Where possible, seek feedback about how you're doing from family or friends and get them to give you their honest opinion.

- **Relax** – What makes charismatic people so charming and likable is how expressive they are with their bodies. They don't stand there in the middle of a conversation, stiff as a board, looking uncomfortable. They are expressive, but in just the right amount so as not to go overboard. When you're in a social setting, relax. Immerse yourself in the conversation and forget about everything else. Express enthusiasm and gesture appropriately where relevant. This too can be practiced in front of the mirror when you're holding pretend conversations with yourself. When doing so, take note of how you appear. Are you nodding too much? Are your shoulders and arms too stiff? Are you gesturing too much? Are you crossing your arms in front of your body without realizing it? Gesturing may not seem like such a big deal, but remember in a social setting, when you're dealing with people who are different from you, small actions can be perceived differently. It is never a good idea to assume that everyone is going to think like you and understand where you're coming from. If you want to improve your charismatic skills, you need to start practicing these moves in the mirror. Again, ask the opinions and seek the feedback of others in your trusted social circle. This is the best way to gauge if your efforts are working and paying off. Consider watching videos or Ted Talks of successful individuals and motivational speakers to study how they express themselves with their bodies.

- **The Person You're Talking to Matters** – And you need to make them feel that way. Being charismatic is not just about focusing on yourself (high emotional intelligence, remember?); it's about making the people that you are engaged with feel just as important. Would you like to be in a conversation with someone who does not make you feel valued? Or someone that makes you feel like your ideas are a bore? Definitely not, and therein lies your answer about how to become more charismatic. All you have to do is make them feel special. Give them your undivided attention. Smile. Be excited when you talk to them. Respect them. Treat them like an equal (nobody should ever be made to feel like they are below or beneath you; it's about mutual respect). Make them feel important by asking open-ended questions and encourage them to talk about themselves. Listen when they speak. Nod when you agree with what they're saying. Make brief interjections where appropriate during a conversation which shows that you are clearly listening. Even something as simple as, *Yes, I completely agree,* is enough to reassure them that you are listening. That is all the charismatic magic that you need to win at improving your charisma.

Social skills and charisma are essential skills that you can begin developing and working on together with your emotional intelligence. It is not as difficult as it may seem to become someone who is charming and comfortable in any kind of social setting that they are thrown into. It takes consistent practice. Be confident and do your best every time, and if there are instances where someone doesn't like you or get along with you, that's okay. There are billions of people in the world; it would be impossible to get along with every single one of them. The point is just to do your best, be as genuine as you can, and be confident.

Chapter 8: Empath Empowerment

What springs to your mind when you think of the word *empath*? Do you believe that empaths are people who have already been born with that gift? That's a common misconception, although true in some cases. However, being an empath is truly (like everything else we have learned so far in this book) a skill that you can learn.

Becoming an empath is about training your mind and exercising it to become more attuned to empathy. It is about shifting your mindset and training it until empathy becomes second nature to you.

Empathy is one of the core concepts of becoming an individual with high emotional intelligence because:

- It further enhances your ability to relate and understand those around you.
- It helps you resolve conflicts better and manage disagreements when you can empathize with others.
- It helps you accurately predict how others are going to react.
- It makes you more confident at expressing your point of view because you're attuned to your surroundings.
- Others will view you as a source of comfort, sometimes even as someone who can heal them emotionally.
- It improves your motivation to become better and to thrive in any social setting.

- You form better and stronger bonds with the relationships that you forge, even the new ones.
- You will find it much easier to forgive others because you can see things from their perspective, reflect on why they reacted that way, and understand where they're coming from.
- It makes you more aware of your non-verbal body language and the way you come across to others.

Why Empathy Is Important

If you want to wield any kind of influence, you need to have empathy on your team. Without being able to sense the way that others feel, you'll find it an uphill task to leave any kind of positive impression on them.

When you fail to sense the way that others around you feel, your social interactions will suffer as a result. You will find it very difficult to build effective rapports – and even to form solid bonds. People must be able to like you, trust you, and relate to you if they are going to allow themselves to be influenced by you.

A skilled empath is someone who is effective at reading emotional cues. They can listen effectively to the voices of the people around them because they have a genuine understanding of where that person is coming from.

How to Become an Empath

Since empathy is one of the core elements of emotional intelligence, it is only fitting that we do what we must towards building our empath abilities. To become an empath, start with the following strategies:

- **Connect with Yourself** – Before you can begin understanding, you must first connect with yourself. An effective empath is someone who is centered – someone who is down-to-earth and grounded. When you are connected with yourself, you're less likely to become distracted easily by what's going on around you. You're able to focus on what matters at hand. One of the best techniques you could apply to connect with yourself is meditation.
  - Meditation helps you find balance, calm and inner peace, and it can be utilized in almost every aspect of your life whenever you feel anxious, worried or stressed. Learning to control our minds is one of the most difficult things we can do. But to become an empath, this is what is needed. It's easy to let our thoughts and emotions get the best of us. It is so easy to be consumed by negativity. Learning to become an empath begins within you, and you start by learning how to focus and gain control of what's happening internally.
  - Another method you could use to connect with yourself is to spend a few minutes every day just being in your own company. We live in a society today that is far too

attached to their technological devices, and it is time we ditched them for a bit. You'll never connect with yourself if your eyes are constantly glued to a digital screen. Pause, take a breath, slow down, and just appreciate being with yourself. This can be done along with your meditation sessions. It gives you time to reflect on what matters to you, and more importantly, it gives you a few minutes to clear your head and think.

- **Putting Yourself in Their Shoes** – This is perhaps the most obvious thing that you can do, but it works. Whenever you're involved in a conversation with someone, always picture what it would be like to see things from their point of view, not just yours. This is one of the most basic yet effective ways which you can begin growing your empathy skills. We may not realize it, however, rarely do we ever give proper thought to what someone else might be going through. We may listen to what they're telling us, and we may sympathize. But how often do we attempt to *feel* what they're currently dealing with?
    - You may have been guilty in the past of brushing someone off as just being silly, or dramatic or exaggerating way too much. That's what happens when we lack the necessary empathy skills to respond appropriately. It may be silly or dramatic to us, but to them, it could be a very serious matter. Being an empath will teach you to see beyond your own feelings and connect to someone else without prejudice or judgment.

- **Give More Thought to Them** – When you're eating that delicious lunch you just bought from the store nearby, do you think about the people who worked hard to prepare it for you? The hours that they spent in the kitchen, so you didn't have to? When you're enjoying your delicious cup of coffee at the local coffee shop, do you think about the ones who went through all that trouble to gather the coffee beans that you're enjoying right now? The people who helped to ship and deliver that coffee to the local shop where you're sitting at this moment enjoying the fruits of their labor? Giving the people around you deeper thought is an approach that you could use to begin training your empathy skills. These people do not necessarily have to be directly in front of you for you to make the connection. It is about taking a moment to think about these people and silently offering them a quick thank you. It is about connecting with humanity.

- **Eliminate Prejudices** – This can be a tough one. A lot of us are prejudice without even realizing it. For others, being prejudice is already an innate part of who they are. When someone of a different race, gender or religion approaches you, how do you react if it is something you're unfamiliar with? Do you automatically set up a barrier? That's being prejudice, and it is what's going to prevent you from becoming an empath if you don't work to get rid of it. To become an empath, you are going to have to challenge your prior beliefs and the prejudices you currently have. Work to get rid of them and start to view people, places, and situations with an open mind. Just because a person is different from you doesn't mean you should be wary. Everyone is still human at the end of the day. Get rid of the barriers and start viewing everyone as only one thing – human. We're all equals on this earth, and we should mutually respect one another. To help you with this, try to find something which you can connect on. Some common ground. This helps you focus on the things which make you similar, and less on what makes you different. When you can relate to them and connect on a shared interest, you'll have a greater interactive experience, and eventually, boundaries will just slip away. This is when greater empathy occurs, by opening up to the people around you and welcoming them as part of your circle.

- **Curiouser and Curiouser** – As we grow older, we tend to keep to ourselves and want to disconnect from the world, especially if we're not naturally social individuals. However, if you want to become an empath, you're going to need to start nurturing your curiosity again. Start getting curious about people. Look for reasons to engage with people you normally wouldn't connect with. Strike up conversations with people who come from different backgrounds than you do. By socializing with a diverse group of individuals and casting your net far and wide, you develop a more universal understanding of the world and people around you. It helps you see these individuals as humans and break down any further barriers which might have existed that prevented you from being more empathetic with them.

Being an empath is not just a skill for someone who was born with that natural gift; it is something we all can learn. Emotional intelligence and empathy are not just about working on controlling and understanding emotions; it is about learning to *act, be and care*. These should slowly start to become part of your personality. By simply changing your attitude, displaying a little love and care, you would be surprised at what a world of difference it can make.

How to Be More Self-Disciplined When It Comes to Your Emotions

To do this, you need to change your mindset and enforce a lot of self-discipline. Changing your mindset can do wonders to transform your life and your emotions. Developing the right mindset can become the most powerful tool you will have. It will get you from where you are right now to where you want (or hope) to be in your life (which is to become an empath with high levels of EQ).

Gandhi once said, "You need to be the change that you wish to see in the world," and this couldn't be truer. If you want to see real change happening in your life, and in ways you never thought possible, it all starts with you. The kind of mindset that you have is a reflection of your current emotional intelligence levels. Do you think it could be time to change your mindset? The answer is yes if you can relate to any of the following signs below.

Five Signs That It's Time to Change Your Mindset

Our thoughts can hurt us more than we know. More importantly, they can affect our emotions in such a significant way that we end up reacting in the way that we know we shouldn't. The problem with a negative mindset is that it acts like an anchor that weighs you down, and it means that your emotional intelligence levels still need some working on.

- **Do You Find It Hard to Let Go?** – Especially the mistakes and the failures that you've faced. To become an empath that possesses high EQ, you are going to need to shift this train of thought, or emotional freedom is something which is always going to elude you.

- **Do You Always Feel Demotivated?** – You find yourself lacking the desire to do anything, even if it is something as small as meeting a couple of friends for dinner. You feel tired and demoralized, losing any desire even to put in an effort anymore. You find yourself losing that zest for life. This needs to change if you want to work on becoming an empath.

- **Are You Complaining About the Same Thing?** – Like a broken record that keeps repeating, eventually your complaints will start to define you if you don't do something about it. If you find yourself doing this, it is high time you start changing your mindset for the better because no good will ever come out of complaining – except to drive away the people who are close to you. Would you want to be around someone who complains all the time? Definitely not.

- **Do You Make Too Many Excuses?** – There's always going to be a reason not to do something. You prefer to make excuses rather than make an actual effort to change. There's always going to be a reason not to do something; the challenge now is to find reasons *why you should*. Motivation is one of the core concepts of someone with high levels of EQ, and someone like this does not make excuses all the time. They take action instead and become a catalyst for change.

- **Do You Find It Hard to Be Happy?** – No matter how many good things you have to be grateful for, you find yourself feeling unhappy and miserable all the time. Happiness seems like a constant struggle. You may be happy for a while, but it isn't long before you find yourself sinking back into the pit of despair. Time for that mindset to change, my friend.

Let Self-Discipline Be Your Driving Force

You may be wondering if it is still possible to change. Yes, it absolutely is because self-discipline is not a skill set that some people are born with – which is why others have succeeded, and you have not. Self-discipline is a state of mind, and because it is something which can be learned, it can be possessed by anyone with the desire to cultivate it and make it a part of who they are. This tool is going to be your driving force towards gaining better control over your emotions once and for all.

There is no easy way or shortcut towards gaining more self-discipline. You are going to have to put in time, effort, and energy into the entire process if you want to make it happen. To become the disciplined person that you want to be, to make the positive changes in your life that you hope to see, it is going to require some sacrifices on your part.

Adjustments need to be made, and there are going to be some difficult things you might have to do, but change is necessary for the greater good, and this has to be a sacrifice you must be willing to make. Everyone can learn how to build a healthy self-discipline habit. It is simply up to you whether you choose to do it or not (hopefully you do!). Once you do, you will be amazed at the momentous effect it will have on your life, and what a difference it can make.

Here's how you can improve your self-discipline levels, and use this trait to change your mindset and improve your control over your emotions:

- **Be Persistent** – Having the intention to become a more self-disciplined person alone is not enough if you are not willing to keep that momentum going, which is why persistence is another important trait that you need to build as part of your character. Your success will depend upon your ability to persist even when the odds are not in your favor. Setbacks will happen, wrenches will be thrown in your plan, and in the face of all that, you must persist with self-discipline to see you through.

- **Practice Time Management** – Time management is one of the most important skills you can master, and it is in this area where self-discipline is the most important. Why? Because the way that you manage your time will determine the outcome of the life that you lead. Time is its own master, and while you may not be able to manage or control it, you can certainly control what you do with your time. Start making the most out of your time by choosing to spend it differently. Where previously you might have wasted much of it doing menial things that were not going to benefit you in the long term, or even if you barely got anything done at all because you procrastinated and found excuses not to get to it thanks to a lack of self-discipline, you need to do a complete turnaround and start spending it very differently.

- **Changing Your Habits** – Building healthy, productive habits is the first step to changing your life. Why do your habits need to change when all you want to acquire is more self-discipline? Because everything that you do is going to affect you both mentally and physically. While self-discipline may be a productive skill to have, if it is weighed down by all your negative habits, it is eventually going to drag you down with it.

- **Set Goals** – For self-discipline to turn your life around, it is important that you first find your mission and have a purpose. Set a goal for yourself, and it does not even have to be anything tremendous right away. You could always start with a small goal that you are working towards achieving and then build momentum from there. You must write down this goal or mission because it will help you clearly define what it is you need to accomplish. When something is physically there in front of you, it makes it real as opposed to simply having several random thoughts and ideas in your head that you may forget along the way. Write it down and stick it somewhere that you will see it every day without fail.

Chapter 9: Leadership and Emotional Intelligence

Why are some people more successful than others? What is it that makes them leaders who stand out in the crowd? Their work ethic and personality could be contributing factors, but that is only part of the story. The other is the *emotional intelligence* that they possess. In simpler terms, think of EQ as being *street smart*. This is the quality that enables you to navigate through life effectively, and this is the exact quality that you need to develop if you want to find yourself in a leadership position one day.

A successful leader and manager is one that can bring out the best in everyone that they work with. When you have emotional intelligence, it shows. You're more confident, determined, passionate, hardworking, and flexible to the point that you can readily adapt when the situation calls for it. You think on your feet, recover quickly from stress, and remain calm even in the most challenging situations. Being a leader is not an enviable position. There's a huge responsibility that comes with it, and when something goes wrong, you are the one that people turn to for answers and solutions.

The Characteristics of Someone with High EQ

There is no company out there that can succeed without the right kind of leadership at the helm. Being a leader is very different from being an *effective and successful* leader; one is going to be the head of a company that will just be mediocre, but the other will head a company that is destined for success.

A leader with high emotional intelligence displays the following qualities:

- **They Love Meeting New People** – They have cultivated their curiosity to the point that they never shy away from meeting new people. In fact, they have come to love it. They ask many questions, make a person feel at ease and welcomed, exhibit empathy, and are attuned to the feelings of the other person – even if they may be strangers. This is what someone with high EQ looks like.

- **They Are Attentive** – High EQ individuals are not easily distracted. They are focused, and they can see the bigger picture. They rarely settle for instant gratification. They are attentive and present to their current situation, themselves, and the people that surround them. This is self-awareness in play. They can focus and concentrate on what they are supposed to do, and they do not stop until the goal has been accomplished – no matter the obstacle.

- **They Know Their Strengths** – High EQ enables the ability to be honest with yourself. Exceptional leaders know their strengths and weaknesses, and they embrace both of these with open arms. They don't make excuses for their weakness; they find ways to work on improving them. Not only can they identify their own strengths and weaknesses, but they can also do the same for others that they work with. In a team setting, they know how to identify each team member's area of strength and use that to benefit the team.

- **They Know Why They're Upset** – Leaders always know exactly what the emotional problem is. Not just in themselves, but in others too. This is because they have fine-tuned their self-awareness ability to recognize their emotions so well that they can always recognize *why* they may be upset. They have developed the ability to recognize these emotions as they come up and identify them accurately. Moreover, because they are emotionally intelligent, they can take a step back and make an objective reflection about how the emotion is affecting them.

- **When They Fall, They Rise Again** – A leader never gives up. It is the way that they deal with mistakes which says a lot about what high EQ can do for a person. They know that giving up is never an option, and they know what it takes to get back on the horse and keep marching forward. They are resilient, determined, and never entertain negative emotions because they know it is only a distraction. They never let their motivation dwindle, thanks to high EQ.

- **They Create a Safe Space** – Leaders understand that everyone needs to feel comfortable enough to voice their opinions and concerns. If they are having difficulty working with someone else, they need to feel comfortable enough to approach you – the leader – and bring up those concerns without worrying that there are going to be repercussions for themselves. As a leader, you need to establish yourself as a trustworthy figure and encourage an open-door policy among the people you are managing – encouraging them and making them feel safe whenever they approach you with a problem of their own (knowing that you are not going to use that information against them in the future).

How to Use Emotional Intelligence to Lead Effectively

A leader of a successful company is one that can effectively manage their team and bring out the best in everyone that is under their guidance. A successful leader and manager is one that can bring out the best in everyone that they work with. A good leader is one that knows how to spearhead the journey to success.

Use emotional intelligence to become an effective leader by:

- **Displaying Mutual Respect** – Respect is one of the major principles that absolutely must be present within a team and an organization. Respect among managers and co-workers is the glue that keeps the company successful, and without it, things can unravel really quickly. Use empathy, self-awareness and social skills to help you foster mutual respect. The best type of leaders are ones that provide a work environment where employees help each other and value the contributions that each individual makes. Effective leaders constantly encourage their peers to bring their A-game to work every day and help them overcome the challenges faced at the workplace without belittling them.

- **Welcoming Diversity** – If you want to be an effective leader that solves problems for good, you need to tailor your solutions depending on the person you are dealing with. Self-awareness, empathy and social skills again come into play here. Use this high EQ trait to treat the individuals in your team just as they are – individuals.

- **Effectively Managing Conflict** – If there is one thing that nobody wants to deal with, it is conflict, especially conflict in the workplace because it really brings down morale and leads to very unhappy staff if not dealt with accordingly. Nobody wants to deal with conflict, but as a leader, you are going to have to. A leader with high EQ is going to depend on empathy, self-regulation, self-awareness, and social skills to help them with this. An effective leader will never turn a blind eye to conflict and will do everything in their power to address the conflict as soon as it rears its ugly head and resolve it in the most amicable way possible.

- **Engaging with People** – When you engage with your team members, as a leader, you need to go the extra mile and make a connection with each member of your team. This helps build a connection that is meaningful and shows your team members you genuinely care about them and their welfare – not just because it is part of your job to do so. Rely on social skills, empathy, and self-awareness for this category.

- **Recognize Each Person for What They Are** – In a work environment especially, sometimes a leader can be so focused on expecting employees to be more like them that they forget to appreciate what makes that employee unique. There is nothing that demotivates a team quicker than feeling like they are not appreciated. When they begin to feel demotivated, they begin to lose the passion and the drive to really strive to perform. An effective leader will use their emotional intelligence skills (social and empathy) to recognize each employee's contribution and work with them on developing their individual strengths. They recognize each employee for what they are, and they never expect them to be something that they are not.

- **Making Trust a Priority** – Without trust, there is no possibility of working together well. For a leader to be considered successful, they must cultivate an environment of trust at all times. You are leading others who have placed their faith in you, and you should return that faith by being as transparent, honest and open as possible. Use social skills and empathy as your guiding points, learn how to read the emotions of others well, and you will have no problems making trust a priority.

- **Being Empathic Always** – A successful leader is one who can practice empathy and compassion with sincerity. High EQ skills will enable you to do this. People are more acute at spotting insincerity than you think, no matter how good of an actor you think you are. Part of being a transparent leader means being honest not just verbally, but also with your feelings too.

- **Listening Actively** – A successful leader is one that has learned to listen intently, and not just to what the person has to say, but beyond that. For example, when having a one-on-one conversation, listen to the voice inflections, the tone of the person's voice, which words they emphasize on, and how they sound when they are expressing what they feel. This is where empathy is going to play a huge role because it is a valuable high EQ skill which is going to help you really connect with the person you're speaking to. Be emphatic towards them, compassionate, understanding and nurturing in a way that they really need. Don't just listen to what they are saying, but listen to what they are trying to tell you and tune in to them in a way many leaders fail to do today.

How Emotional Intelligence Can Increase Your Chances of Success

To improve the quality of your life, you need to have emotional intelligence on your side. This is the key trait of making a difference. No shortcuts. No secret weapons. No magic formulas. Just developing high levels of EQ.

To achieve success in general, here is how EQ is going to play a huge role in helping you achieve that. How often have you set goals, raised the bar, and had big dreams only to have life getting in the way? Your emotions get worked up through stress, and all your initial desire to succeed just comes crashing to a halt. When someone lacks EQ, they tend to become more reactive than proactive. They are unable to adapt to the situations as they come. The experiences affect them more than they should, and they become far too overwhelmed by the wave of emotions that crash around them. This is precisely why you need EQ.

EQ trains you to manage your emotions in healthy ways. It enables you to reign in impulsive behaviors, manage your expectations and adapt to the unexpected that happens. *This* is how you succeed. The ability to understand your emotions is half the EQ battle, and if you can achieve this portion, you've already won (almost). The other half is, of course, learning how to understand and manage the emotions of other people. Obstacles are the biggest reason many fail to reach the goals they have set, because the challenges, the setbacks, disappointments, and failure can often strip you of the will you need to keep going – especially if you don't know how to regulate your emotions.

Here are other ways emotional intelligence can increase your chances of success:

- **It Helps You Predict Performance** – EQ has a large impact on success because it helps you focus on results which matter. When you focus on the results, your performance is instantly given a boost, and thanks to self-awareness, you will be able to predict your actions and reactions to the situations you may be facing.

- **It Leaves No Room for Negativity** – When you've got high EQ, there is no room for anything that may threaten your success, which includes negativity. Think of negativity like you would your garbage, and if garbage is not something you would willingly put into your mind, why are you allowing negative thoughts to creep in there?

- **It Makes You Hungry for Success** – To be successful, you need to be hungry for it, long for it. Be so hungry that you'd be willing to do anything you could just to satisfy that hunger. Imagine a similar scenario where you haven't eaten all day, and you're starving for a bite to eat. That's how you need to approach the concept of success. As we have already established, high EQ individuals never lose sight of their motivation, and they use their self-awareness and self-regulation to manage their emotions when they are faced with difficult circumstances. This ensures that the desire to quit is never stronger than the desire for success.

- **It Helps You Be Mindful** – It is all about being attuned to emotions. That is EQ at the core. It is important to be mindful of your emotions if you want to become successful. Being mindful simply means being aware of the thoughts that pop into your head and taking control of those thoughts. By being mindful of the thoughts that creep into your head, you're instantly more attuned to what those thoughts are and how they make you feel. If it isn't good for you, kick it right out of your mind where it belongs.

- **It Helps You Minimize Stress** – Life can be very stressful, especially because you can't seem to find any reason to be happy and it feels like the weight of the world is on your shoulders. With so much internal burden to carry around, how would you focus on achieving success? This is why high EQ makes a difference – because of how it helps you regulate your emotions and manage them properly. Minimizing your stress means you will now have the mental clarity that is needed to start thinking about the next step you need to take.

- **It Improves Your Self-Esteem** – Something that so many of us struggle with. It is impossible to succeed with low self-esteem because you simply do not believe in yourself enough. Possibly one of the best benefits of improving your EQ is how much it is going to improve your self-esteem in the long run. When you begin to constantly pursue betterment in your life, you'll find more things to be happy about, which leads to higher levels of satisfaction – improving the way you feel about yourself and thereby enhancing your self-esteem. The constant pursuit of betterment is an example of you succeeding in life in general.

- **It Makes It Easier to Spot Opportunities** – Being self-aware has so many benefits, and not just because it helps you manage your emotions better. When you are more attuned to your surroundings, yourself and the people around you, it becomes easier to notice the opportunities that you may not otherwise have spotted. Negativity and a lack of EQ often cloud our judgment and perception, which is why successful people strive to develop emotional intelligence skills for themselves, so their eyes will be opened to start noticing solutions rather than problems.

- **It Empowers You** – As you learn to manage your emotions better, you start regaining confidence in yourself once more. As your confidence and self-esteem improve, with each challenge you successfully overcome with self-awareness and self-regulation, empathy, motivation, and social skills, you'll find yourself becoming more empowered, stronger, and capable of absolutely anything you set your heart and mind to. You feel like there is nothing that will hold you back, as you see each goal you set materialize before you when you smash through them, and this will serve as your fuel when your build momentum towards transforming your life. This is how EQ helps you succeed in life.

- **It Makes You a Better Version of Yourself** – When you've adopted all the core principles that make high EQ such a desirable trait, without even realizing you're going to put in the effort to become better than what you are right now. You'll start focusing on having a passion and a purpose, and you take the necessary steps that you need to improve the things that you don't want in your life. This is what it means to be successful, to become the best version of yourself that you can possibly be.

- **It Helps You Stay Committed to the End** – Your emotions are no longer in the driver seat when you have high EQ; you are. Giving up is no longer an option because you've learned how to regulate your responses whenever that feeling arises. When you set a goal with high EQ, you're not only creating a goal; you're committing to seeing it through. This commitment is exactly what helps you stay productive because you're able to regulate your emotions to control your reactions and your outcome. Success would not be possible without the desire to be committed to the end.

Chapter 10: All About NLP

Now, we're back to NLP again after touching on it briefly in Chapter 4. As you already know, NLP is Neuro-Linguistic Programming, and it has three components. The neuro component focuses on neurology, linguistic refers to language, and programming is about using neural language functions. NLP, in other words, means learning the language of your mind. Isn't that an interesting thing?

Created in the 1970s in California by Richard Bandler and John Grinder, NLP courses are now introduced in seminars and by companies looking to train their managers to enhance their skills in communication and better governance.

Understanding NLP

Just to reinforce the concept of NLP again, let's take a look at another scenario. Imagine trying to communicate with someone who doesn't speak your language and can't understand you no matter how hard you try to explain things – it's like trying to order a dish in a foreign country where you don't speak the language. What we order and what actually comes to our table are two different things.

This is the kind of partnership that most of us have with our unconscious mind. We think something, but what happens, in reality, is a different story altogether. In the practice of NLP, the conscious mind is the goal-setter, whereas the unconscious mind is the goal-getter. The unconscious mind should not be seen as a troublemaker. It is there to get you what you want in life – your goals, tasks, and needs. However, if you do not know how to communicate with what you want in life, then the result is often the opposite of what you desire.

In short, NLP is a personal development tool that is created to help people have better relationships with themselves and the people around them in the pursuit of their goals and happiness – to ultimately lead a more meaningful life.

What are the benefits of NLP?

Before we move into the techniques and practices of NLP, it is also wise to explore the benefits of NLP in both life, work, and relationships. Here is a breakdown of what you can expect when you go through NLP courses:

In your career:

- By knowing your goals and staying focused on them, you will eventually develop an edge on your competition in business – this can safely and systematically increase your profits.
- If you manage a team, you will learn to effectively manage your internal mindset so that it can positively influence the people you work with, eventually forming a happy and conducive working environment for your entire team to enable them to achieve the team goals.
- NLP also helps you overcome hurdles that may prevent you from taking your career or your business to the next level of greatness.
- You will also learn to motivate yourself as well as the people around you, especially at times of crisis.
- By using a better way to communicate, you will create greater elegance and precision so that you and your team can get what you want to attain your goals.
- You will also learn to think better, be more focused, have better clarity and make constructive decisions.

In your life:

- NLP practice and techniques enable you to connect with yourself and your relationships in a more enriching way.
- You will also be open to more learning possibilities, be more adapted to the changes happening in your life and learn as life moves on.
- Your ability to immediately identify and push through your limitations will also increase. You will also gain a higher momentum of motivation to continue pursuing your business objectives as well as your life mission. Once you break through these limitations, both your life and business will never be the same again as it will change for the better.
- NLP will also train you to master your unconscious mind to learn more quickly than conventional teaching methods allow.

- As you continue practicing NLP, you also learn plenty of things about yourself that you never knew and also discover skills you never thought you had, and increase the creative side of your brain.

- Along the way, you will be more adept at steering your emotions, so they do not get the better of you. You will learn to handle your emotions according to the situation you are in.

- Become a more effective and powerful communicator because you now have a vital edge.

- Your personal relationships will be enhanced as you get better at empathizing and understanding a person's perspective of scenarios.

- You will also work towards increasing your confidence and self-esteem.

NLP and Emotional Intelligence

Neuro-Linguistic Programming is the user's manual of the brain. Training yourself in NLP greatly improves your emotional intelligence and it teaches you how to connect with the language of your mind, understanding your mind as well as how someone else's mind could think. It also helps us connect mindfully with our unconscious mind so that we will have a better understanding of what we want out of life.

Through NLP training, it helps us have better communication with ourselves and with others. The tools and techniques in NLP not only trains us to be better communicators but it also alters our attitudes towards achieving our goals and getting the results we want.

Using NLP to Build Emotional Intelligence

Registered psychologist and NLP practitioner, Miriam Henke, says that using NLP on Emotional Intelligence is the ability to recognize, use and manage emotions in constructive and positive ways. It also makes us better equipped at recognizing the emotional state of other people and engaging with them effectively in a way that is mutually beneficial, safe and trustworthy for all.

Using NLP techniques and practices enables us to enhance our emotional intelligence so that it can facilitate improvement in relationships, build authentic partnerships and create meaningful connections, especially with the groups of people we find the hardest to connect with such as colleagues, bosses, team members, clients, and suppliers.

As we know from previous chapters, emotional intelligence is a skill that can be learned and developed. This can be done by taking ownership of our emotions and enhance our relationships by becoming positive influences, not only to others but also to ourselves.

Here are some of the ways NLP is used in building Emotional Intelligence:

- Increasing our self-awareness – through this, NLP teaches us to understand the way our mind works and how our emotional state, moods, and thoughts impact our behavior and the result of it.

- Shifting our feelings – a technique used in NLP called Anchoring enables us to recognize a more resourceful and practical mood and emotional state. This technique also shows us that our physiological state also affects our mood.

- Using Self Talk – our self-talk is with our inner voice, which all of us have that is either an inner critic or a cheerleader. With NLP, we can program that inner voice so that it doesn't get in the way of being an obstacle or acting in a way that goes against our goals, beliefs, and tasks.

- Creating strategies for better self-management – people with good EQ are generally more aware of their internal pressure scale, and they also have a better coping mechanism than those with lower EQ. With NLP, the idea here is to become better managers of ourselves concerning our moods, behaviors, and emotions.

- Building Better Rapport – having a good rapport is good for better partnerships, especially at work. Without rapport, there is no communication. One of the biggest traits that you can cultivate is being a better listener. NLP courses teach people to listen better to empathize rather than to formulate an answer.

- Building Empathy – using the NLP technique called Perceptual Positions, we can see a person's point of view which gives us better and new insight. This will help us build empathy with the people around us, especially our family, friends, and colleagues.

Practical Exercises to Enhance Your Emotional Intelligence

Speaking of practices and techniques, here are some of the more practical ones that you can try on your own to build EQ using NLP practices:

#1 Dissociation

Dissociation is the technique of identifying an emotion or feeling that makes us feel nervous or fearful and removing it entirely. You may have been in a situation where you suddenly have a bad feeling, but this isn't about instinct or gut feeling. Rather, the experience just mentally breaks you down, such as giving a speech in front of people or even taking the elevator alone (some people feel uncomfortable being in a small space). Maybe you suddenly retract from conversations when you feel surrounded by people? These feelings may seem like a normal reaction, but while it is okay to feel this way sometimes, it can be chronic if it starts interfering in life and work. The dissociation technique helps to overcome this feeling and involves:

1. Identifying the emotions that you want to overcome.

2. Imagine yourself floating out of your body to look at yourself and look at the entire scenario from an observer's point of view.

3. Notice how you feel.

4. Imagine flowing out of your body again, so you are looking at yourself, looking at yourself. This double take on dissociation usually gets rid of any negative emotion from a minor situation.

#2 Content Reframing

This technique is extremely useful whenever we feel helpless or when negative thoughts and emotions come weighing down at us. Reframing basically involves taking a negative situation and empowering yourself by changing the meaning that you associate the experience with, subsequently turning it into a positive experience.

It starts with:

1. Identifying the negative scenario such as a divorce. Divorces are never easy but let's reframe it.

2. What are the positive outcomes of being divorced? You can now look at other relationships. You can also look forward to forming a better relationship with the next person since you have learned valuable lessons. You have the freedom to do the things you couldn't do while being in the previous relationship.

3. You have taken a negative scenario and reframed it to give yourself an entirely different experience.

4. Shifting your focus to more positive aspects just helps you have better clarity; thus, enabling you to make better decisions.

#3 Anchoring

As described earlier, anchoring is a very significant and commonly used NLP technique. Anchoring is best described as a neurological association between a sound, scenario or situation and the behavior we have when we come face-to-face with that situation. It is also known as a conditioned response. In NLP, it is simply described as anchoring yourself to these situations.

Anchoring helps us have a desired positive emotional response when we face a certain sensation. When we choose a positive emotion or thought, and connect it deliberately to a simple gesture, we also trigger the anchor whenever we feel negative emotions. This technique is meant to change our emotions immediately. It involves:

1. Starting with identifying how we want to feel whether it is calmness or happiness or even confidence.

2. Deciding where this feeling should be placed to anchor our body. It can be a small place like our earlobe or even clasping our fingers, rubbing our palms or simply touching our knuckles. The physical action allows us to trigger our positive sensations at will. It doesn't

matter where this physical action is as long as when you do it, it is unique to you and you know what it means.

3. Go back into your past at a time when you felt that state of feeling and mentally float your body to the time you felt most confident or happy or calm. Look at this scenario through your own eyes and relive that memory. Slowly adjust your body language so that it matches that memory. Experience what you see and hear what you heard back in this memory as well as the feeling that came into you.

4. This experience is the same as recollecting a funny joke or story from the past and the feelings you felt and the memories you experienced. Anchoring is getting into this experience and feeling the happiness you felt.

5. Cling as much as you can onto this memory through touching, pulling and squeezing the part of your body of your choosing. Release from the touch when the emotional state peaks and starts wearing off.

6. What you are doing is creating a neurological stimulus-response which will trigger the state of emotions whenever you touch yourself at the spot again. Whether it is confidence or happiness or calmness, touching this spot again will trigger your positive responses.

7. To enhance the memory or response trigger, think of another memory that you felt and relive it again by going through this anchoring practice again. Each time you add your anchor of positive feelings, the trigger will be stronger.

#4 Creating Better Rapport

This NLP technique is easy but extremely powerful to help get along with just about anyone. While there are plenty of ways to build rapport, this NLP technique is the most effective, not to mention the quickest. It involves mirroring, very subtly, the other person's body language and tone of voice. Easy but needs to be done with extreme subtlety – that you can almost consider it art. People generally like other people who are like themselves – birds of a feather flock together anyway. By mirroring the other person's actions, the brain gives off mirror neurons, which are pleasure sensors that give people the sense of liking someone that is mirroring them.

Here's what you need to do:

1. Stand or sit the way the other person is standing or sitting. Tilt your head the same way.

2. Smile when they smile. Mirror their facial expressions and their body language.

3. The idea here is to do it as unconsciously and subtly as possible.

Do not be too overt as then it may seem like you are merely copying them and this will break rapport. Mirror people in a calm and natural way.

#5 Influence and Persuasion

NLP practices are especially dedicated to helping people to manage conflict, eliminate negative emotions, as well as do away with limiting beliefs. A small portion of NLP, though, is dedicated to influencing and persuading other people.

Milton H. Erickson, a mentor in the NLP field who is also a psychiatrist, studied the subconscious mind using hypnotherapy – the scientific line not the entertainment kind. Erickson was adept at hypnosis, and he also created a way to speak to the subconscious minds of people without even needing hypnotism. He could also hypnotize people at any given time. This method that Erickson used became known as Conversational Hypnosis.

Conversational hypnosis is a powerful tool that can be used to not only persuade and influence people but also to help people overcome fears, manage conflicts, stop limiting beliefs and raise conscious awareness.

Conclusion

NLP provides a variety of set techniques and tools that can be applied to different aspects of our lives. For anyone learning them and using them in day-to-day interactions, it can greatly improve the quality of our lives, as well as the relationships we have with the people we communicate with on a daily basis.

Not only does NLP improve communication, but it also increases our goal-reaching and the outcomes that take place from the interactions we conduct. It also allows us to overcome obstacles – both professional and personal, as well as psychological problems. These techniques help us use tools we already have but just never realized we had in us.

When we learn these techniques, we are one step away from positively changing our lives and the lives of people around us, and we also get closer to achieving our goals.

Conclusion

Thank you for making it through to the end of this book. It should have been informative and provided you with all of the tools you need to achieve your goals – whatever they may be.

Now, there is only one thing left to do: use the tools you've been given. Everything you just read is what you need to get started on improving your emotional intelligence. You need to use the tools as you see fit and realize that these tools are here to help you.

Every piece of information in this book serves a purpose. Try your best to utilize all that you have just learned, and exercise it to some extent in your life from this point forward. The more you practice, the better you will become. Seeing a difference in your emotional intelligence begins with you.

If this journey is your first step, don't worry – we've all been there. The best advice is to start small by choosing three goals that you would like to focus on for the next week. Choose one or two (maybe more, depending on what you feel) simple actions, which you could begin practicing to give your emotional intelligence a boost. Even better, put them into action in your daily life. Once you've gained enough confidence through several practice sessions, choose another tool or technique to focus on. Keep repeating the process.

Emotional intelligence is something that takes practice. It takes time to build –sometimes years. Even then, you could make mistakes along the way. The important thing is not to let setbacks discourage you. We're only human – mistakes are a part of life. What matters is how well you pick yourself up again and keep persevering. Be patient as you work towards building your emotional intelligence to a point you're proud of. This is a long-term journey, and you may not notice it along the way, but you will be amazed by how far you've come when you look back on it one day.

Finally, if you found this book useful in any way, a review on Amazon is always appreciated!

Thanks for your support!

Part 2: Anger Management

How to Control Anger, Master Your Emotions, and Eliminate Stress and Anxiety, including Tips on Self-Control, Self-Discipline, NLP, and Emotional Intelligence

Introduction

Anger. An unpleasant emotion which can lead to equally unpleasant consequences if left unchecked. Generally speaking, anger is an extreme emotional response to something that disturbs us. We feel antagonism and strong irritation because something has gone wrong and there seems to be unkind intent from a perpetrator and a desire to cause us harm. Anger is mostly directed toward those we know – friends, family, coworkers – and usually, the expression of it is vocal. Aggression, the violent element that is sometimes a part of anger is less common, although it does exist. The question is how do we control it?

The problem with anger is that in some instances, for some individuals, it is difficult to control. It can turn into road rage, a boardroom yelling match, or a wrongful death suit directed at a doctor who really wasn't culpable. In fact, the worst thing about moderate anger isn't what it makes us do to others, but the negative influence it can have on the person whose anger goes uncontrolled. How many of us have fired off an email at a perceived insult, only to discover we misunderstood the point or didn't have all the information needed to understand what was going on? That is the anger we need to learn to control, and there are methods and keys in learning to do that.

This guidebook will detail everything that you need to learn regarding how to reign in your anger issues once and for all.

Chapter 1: What is Anger & Where Does It Come From?

Anger is something that is present in everyone. All of us have had moments of "meltdowns" or when we "completely lost it" with friends, family, coworkers, even perfect strangers sometimes. It happens to the best of us. It only becomes a problem when it happens more frequently than it should and when it happens at extreme levels.

Depending on how you handle it, anger can be something which is both good and bad. When used for good, anger can drive you and motivate you to change for the better. For example, when you see an injustice happening, feeling angry about it fuels your desire to make a change for the better. It can lead to groups that rally and come together for a change to be better like the march for women's rights or animal rights. When anger is used for bad, though, it can lead to terrible things like physical abuse, confrontations that escalate into violence and even worst-case scenarios: murder. Many have gone to jail because they murdered someone in the heat of the moment. That is what happens when anger is left unchecked and out of control. Prolonged anger among friends and families can lead to unhappiness, years of not talking to one another, and ruined relationships.

The problem with anger in some people is that they find it hard to let go. Have you ever had moments where you recalled an argument or a confrontation you had, and the mere thought of it just makes your blood boil all over again? That's what anger can do. It makes you hold onto grudges and unable to forgive, let go and move on.

What is Anger Anyway?

It is one of our core emotions as a human being. Humans are indeed unique creatures, capable of feeling several types of emotions, sometimes even a few emotions at once. Happiness, sadness, joy, anger, disgust, fear, bravery, anxiety, despair, all these are just a small example of the range of emotion we are capable of. It is these emotional states which have helped us survive.

Anger, just like our other emotional states, is used to describe the way that we feel and it helps us identify and connect with what is happening around us. When we are feeling unsafe in a situation, for example, we identify that we're feeling scared or insecure. When something makes us happy, we describe it as joy or happiness. Our emotions are sensitive to what is going on in our surroundings.

Anger is an emotion which has been closely linked to the "fight" or "flight" mechanism which is inbuilt in all of us. It is a way that we respond when we perceive something as a threat. Back when our ancestors were still living and hunting for survival, this emotion helped to keep their minds sharp and simulated, ready for any kind of action.

Where Does It Come From?

Physiologically, we can break down our anger-response to hormonal levels. The amygdala area of the brain triggers response to irritating information or frightening situations. Our "fight or flight" response to annoyances is related to the hormones the brain releases, primarily epinephrine (adrenaline) and norepinephrine (noradrenaline). These hormones result in emotional and physical responses to make us alert and energized. We sometimes call the ensuing sensation an "adrenaline rush" which may lead us to shout obscenities at the judge who is about to determine our prison time, or in extreme fear (an emotion closely related to anger physiologically) lift a heavy tree off of our seven-year-old son. This rush of energy is useful in some situations and probably was even more useful when early humans found themselves face-to-face with a raging beast a bit more often than we do today. So, while managing our anger (and its sister – fear) is important, we wouldn't want to completely disarm the system that sometimes goes into overdrive, causing us to overreact.

Physically, anger can cause other symptoms besides the surge of energy we associate with it. Our hearts often pump faster, and our breathing becomes shallower and quicker. Some people break into a sweat as the blood courses more quickly through their bloodstreams, and rising temperature may lead to the red faces we see in cartoon stereotypes of angry people. While anger is a "hot" emotion, however, fear causes the temperature to decrease – one of the few differences between the body's response to anger and fear.

So that is the physical response to anger, but the psychological response is equally important, and it is our thoughts and behavior that we can adapt to manage anger successfully. Just seeing scratches on our pretty blue car isn't enough to cause an angry outburst for most people. We must also associate someone else with the outcome. Even then, most of us do not act on our anger.

We may vocalize our irritation. "Darn it. I am so tired of that Suburban taking up two spots in the front parking lot! I wish Fred would park where the spots are bigger or get a smaller truck!" We may even fantasize about having the vehicle towed or boxing it in with two other cars. If we don't see or suspect a perpetrator, the response may even shift to sorrow or another emotion. When anger is the appropriate emotional response – when we see that we have been injured, identified a perpetrator, and perceived malice in that act of injury – it is not wrong for us to feel anger. A conversation with Fred about his Suburban may clear the air. However, how we channel that anger may be deeply inappropriate.

When it is justifiable – we watch someone steal our phone or we learn that the promotion we worked hard to earn has been given to a newcomer to the business with a family tied to the CEO – anger makes sense, and the trick is mostly to control the anger and channel it into something more productive than a loud or violent response. That productive path may end up helping us get a better job or perhaps a new and better phone.

What Causes Us to Feel Angry?

Although humans have come a long way and evolved since the time of our ancestors, this emotional state still remains (although it too has evolved since then). The emotional bursts of anger that we feel today still have some similar ties to that of the early humans. For example, when our loved ones are in danger or have been wronged, we feel anger at the perceived threat and want to spring into action to defend them.

In moments of anger, we make poor decisions. We lose all sense of rationale, and our emotional intelligence ceases to exist. All we feel is pure rage (in extreme cases), the blood pounding in our veins, and our muscles become tense and angry. Anger is a raw emotion that can lead you to do things you ordinarily would not do. Anger seems to hijack all our common sense and makes it impossible to make good decisions when we are consumed by this emotion. All we end up doing is either hurting ourselves, the people around us, and feel full of regret with how badly the situation was handled.

There could be several factors which cause you to feel angry. Different people would have different emotional triggers that set off this reaction. Some examples of what could cause a person to feel angry include the following:

- You feel angry when you experience an unfair treatment against you or someone else.
- You feel angry when you are powerless to stop something.
- You feel angry when your goal is not accomplished.
- You feel angry when you think you (or someone else) are being treated unfairly or unkindly.
- You feel angry when promises are broken.
- You feel angry when someone has lied to you.
- You feel angry when you have been disappointed or when you feel disappointed in yourself.
- You feel angry when you are ignored or mistreated.
- You feel angry when you think you're being neglected.
- You feel angry when you experience verbal or physical assault.

- You feel angry when you experience other bad drivers on the road.

- You feel angry when you have to work with colleagues who are either difficult or not on the same page as you are and it is affecting your work.

- You feel angry when you do not get your way (perhaps this is something that you're used to).

Many possible scenarios and situations could cause a person to get angry or upset. One of the things that you need to do towards learning how to manage your anger would be to identify the triggers that set you off so you can then learn to recognize them.

How Do I Know If I Have an Anger Problem?

Do you wonder if your anger ranges in a healthy or unhealthy range? Worried you might have an anger problem? There are several indicators which could help you identify if your anger is indeed something you should be concerned about. How many of the following indicators can you identify with?

- It is hard for you to get over your anger. When you feel angry, you let it simmer and boil within you until it explodes and everyone else around you feels your wrath.

- You can hold a grudge for years because of your anger. You know people whom you have not spoken to for a very long time because you still feel anger towards them.

- You find yourself feeling depressed easily and too frequently, not realizing that this could be a result of repressed anger issues. You find yourself having dangerous suicidal thoughts, perhaps even have tendencies of violence.

- You are unable to express your anger appropriately, choosing instead to bottle it up within you. This could be dangerous too because it may lead to other emotional problems.

- Holding onto your anger is preventing you from living a meaningful, happy life. You constantly find yourself feeling disgruntled, irritated, and frustrated more than you are happy and even the smallest of instances could set you off because of it.

- People have often described you as a very angry individual.

- You're verbally, emotionally (sometimes even physically) abusive towards others around you. You find that it spills over not just into your personal life, but professional life as well.

- You have been called abusive.

- You do not openly express your anger, but you find other ways of channeling it. For example, you're cynical and sarcastic towards yourself or others, or you have adopted a pessimistic outlook on life. This is not a good thing because it can lead to great unhappiness not just for you, but the people around you too.

If far too many of these indicators ring true to you, then you could have a potential anger problem. The first thing you would need to do is accept that your anger is a problem. There is no sense in denying it any longer if you want to fix the situation and learn how to manage your anger better. It needs to begin with acceptance on your part. This is something that no one else can do for you.

You don't have to beat yourself up over it, though, if you do indeed find that you have anger issues. Consider this – *you have valid reasons to be angry*. True, the way that you are expressing that anger may be unreasonable and unacceptable, but you are not getting angry for no reason. You may have good reasons to be angry, but do not use those reasons as an excuse for your behavior. Nothing is ever worth emotionally, verbally, or physically hurting the people around you especially your loved ones. Those kinds of scars can take a long time to heal if they ever do heal at all.

Your anger is triggered by something, and now that you know your reasons, it is time to learn how to manage the second part of the process.

Common Myths about Anger

Before we begin learning how to manage anger better, it is important to break through some of the common myths and misconceptions that you may or may not have regarding anger. This will help develop a deeper understanding of what anger is (and what it isn't), and you will be able to use that understanding to better work on your management techniques.

Here are some of the most common myths about anger that need to be dispelled:

- **Myth – Men are angrier than women.** This is not true as women can be equally as angry as men can. In fact, research has shown that women could get angry just as frequently as men can and both sexes have an equal chance of being just as angry as the other. A man's anger may be more intense than that of a woman, but women can hold onto anger for much longer than a man can.

- **Myth – Anger is only a problem if you show it.** Anger which is not expressed can be just as much of a problem. Repressed anger is similar to how a volcano works. It bubbles and boils under the surface until one day when something sets you off, all that repressed anger just comes shooting out with catastrophic consequences. Anger which is not expressed or shown is just as bad as anger which is blatantly displayed.

- **Myth – The older you get, the angrier you become.** This isn't entirely true. In fact, the older you get for some people, the calmer they are because they know what they want. They know that it simply is not worth it to get angry over trivial matters anymore and they have learned from experience that sometimes it is just not worth getting angry at everything that bugs you.

- **Myth – Anger is a bad thing.** Again, not true, as we described earlier in this book how anger can also be used for good and become a motivating factor. Anger can have many different functions and purposes. It is entirely how you use it. Do you use it to drive you, energize you, or inspire you? Or does it do the complete opposite? That is entirely dependent upon how you handle the situation and your anger.

- **Myth – Anger is all about getting revenge.** That would depend on the individual. This is not true for everyone. For some, revenge is not even something that they think about or getting even could be a secondary motive. It is not always all about revenge, sometimes getting angry is just a way of "venting" or letting out the frustration that has built up within you. For some, their anger only lasts a brief moment, and once it is over, they're back to their old selves not even thinking about it anymore.

- **Myth – Only some "types" of people have anger issues.** This isn't true. Anyone can have anger issues no matter where they come from or what their background may be. It does not necessarily mean that only those who come from broken homes, have a bad record, or non-respectable members of the community have tendencies towards anger problems. Anyone can have anger issues, even that policeman directing traffic on the street or the respectable lawyer working in the city. Grandparents, physicians, homemakers, poor people, rich people, children, professors, scientists. Anyone can be capable of anger issues because anger is an emotion that *everyone* experiences.

Is Anger Affecting Your Health?

Yes. When left unchecked, anger could directly and indirectly affect your health. It is causing health problems without you even realizing it. Some examples of how anger is *indirectly* affecting your health include the following:

- It increases your risks of a heart attack because of the constant stress that you feel.

- It also increases your blood pressure and cholesterol levels, making you prone to having health-related problems because of that stress.

- It could cause obesity (stress-eating, ring a bell?)

And how it is *directly* affecting your health includes:

- Anger affects your decision-making process. You can't make rational, appropriate decisions when you're blinded by anger all the time.

- It drives you to physical injuries. For example, you could punch something in anger which ends up hurting you. Or worst, you could punch someone else which causes physical injury to another person. Neither of which is good, of course.

- Anger could drive some towards alcoholic tendencies.

- Anger could lead to road rage.

- If you drive while you're feeling angry, it makes it difficult to concentrate on your driving which increases the risk of car accidents happening.

These are just a few examples of how anger issues can cause detrimental effects to your health, and you may not even have given it much thought until now – which is why it's now more important than ever that you learn how to manage your anger once and for all.

Chapter 2: Types of Anger Issues – The Good, The Bad, and The Ugly

Some people have a shorter fuse than others, which would explain why they get angry much quicker and more frequently. Often when this happens, there is rarely any time to take control of the situation before it gets out of hand. But why do some people have such a shorter fuse than others? Before we get into the good, bad, and ugly side of anger and what it can lead to, let's take a look at some of the potential reasons behind why you find yourself losing your temper more often than you should. It could be attributed to a number of factors:

•**Your temperament** – Remember how we mentioned that all individuals are unique? This is the perfect example to illustrate that point. We are all different, and therefore, our personalities and our temperaments are different. Not all of us are wired the same way. Some act quicker, while others need more time to process their next move. Some jump to action without thinking twice, while others need more time to ponder the consequences. Some people are more outgoing and adventurous, while some are more laid back and introverted. And in this same way, some people just have a shorter fuse than others do. Our differences are what make us unique.

• **Your personality** – What type of personality would you say you have? Are you generally impatient? Impulsive? Confrontational? Dominating? Bossy? Demanding? Judgmental? If you've answered yes to one or more of these personality traits, then it could explain why you tend to have a shorter fuse than others do. Competitive personalities tend to have shorter fuses too because those with this personality type generally insist or demand that things go their way.

• **The examples you had** – Who were your role models growing up? Did you have parents or other family members who quickly got angry? Sometimes the reason for our short fuses is because that is all we can identify with. That was the example that we had growing up. We don't know any other way because this is how we were raised. If one or both of your parents had a tendency to become angry quickly, chances are you're likely to have that same tendency too.

- **High stress levels** – Are you constantly stressed all the time? Excessive stress which just seems to consume you? You can't even remember a moment when you were *not* feeling stressed. Stress could also act as a potential trigger for a short fuse, leading to abrupt outbursts, temper tantrums, and irrational behavior. It is your body's way of reacting to the stress that you already feel.

- **Do you suffer from mood disorders?** – It could be another reason why you find yourself being angry quickly. An undiagnosed personality disorder could be the trigger for your short fuse without even realizing it. Bipolar disorder, depression, and anxiety are all potential triggers because it won't take much to make you angry. If you do suspect you may have any of these mood disorders, it is best that you seek professional help and don't leave it undiagnosed.

- **Are you getting enough sleep?** – A lack of sleep could also act as a potential trigger for a short fuse. Have you ever noticed how things seem much harder or require more effort when you're feeling tired and fatigued from lack of sleep? You feel cranky, irritable, and even the smallest of things seem like a big deal. That is because your body is tired, your nerves are frayed, and a lack of sleep makes you less efficient than what you normally would be. Therefore, it doesn't take much to set your temper off when you're sleep deprived.

- **How do you view the world?** – What's your outlook on life like? Do you see the world as full of possibilities? Do you wake up each morning with optimism? Or do you have a rather cynical, hostile view of the world around you? The glass is always half empty, and there is no silver lining in sight. When things don't work out the way that you expect them to, it sets off your temper, and you lash out at anything or anyone that may be close by.

- **You have poor communication skills** – When you have a hard time making yourself understood or expressing yourself, it can result in frustration. Poor communication skills can lead to a lot of misunderstanding, which could lead to arguments which cause your temper to rise because you feel like your point is not getting across. Poor communication skills are yet another potential trigger for why you may have a shorter fuse than others.

- **Are you always quick to blame?** – Do you jump at the chance to shift the blame towards someone else? Is it always someone or something that is responsible for your misfortune, never yourself? Do you believe that the "bad" things which happen to you are often a result of someone else's mistakes? Feeling like this all the time is a sure-fire way to a shorter fuse because it makes it so easy to be angry at the world and everyone in it when there is always someone else to blame.

The Good

Earlier in Chapter 1, it was briefly touched on how anger – when used the right way – can be a tool which is used for good. Let's start by looking at some of the positive aspects of our physiological anger response.

Scientists have found more than one advantage to a state of anger. It is short-acting and energizing. It can lead to focus, organization, and clear thinking. Individual results may vary, but since anger is a hormonal response to a specific type of emergency, many people will find that words come to them more easily, their physical strength temporarily increases, and they become minutely and clearly focused on the problem at hand. Professionally, well-channeled anger leads us to seek out solutions and communicate with those who can help instigate change.

When anger is good, and on a healthy level, sometimes it does not even look or feel like anger at all. The occasional irritation is the most that you would feel if your anger was within the healthy range. Good anger will not show up as any kind of aggression at all. This is why anger can sometimes be a good thing. When it is aligned with your values, emotional intelligence, integrity, passion, love, and beliefs, it can motivate you to take positive action without having to rely on aggressive, domineering behavior at all. People who experience healthy anger know that violence and arguments are never the answer, so this is never an option for them.

Anger, when used for good, can spur the following actions:

- It leads you to take precise and direct action
- It motivates you to push past your challenges without perceiving them as a threat
- It gives you the courage to take the necessary action
- It helps you focus on a clear goal
- It awakens your internal fire and passion for making a difference
- It helps you stay in control without the need to explode or lose your temper because you know how to manage your emotions
- It helps you take responsibility for your actions because you understand that blaming someone is never going to do anyone any good
- It empowers you to push past your boundaries and rise to challenges
- It can become one of your greatest assets, pushing you to do what needs to be done

When anger is brought out in intimate relationships, it can result in a discussion of problem areas or lead to creative solutions. Anger at young children is often useful in instigating positive change (mostly in the adult). Since angry adults know they are larger than their children and could hurt or frighten them with a loud or physical response, most angry parents are careful to harness their angry feelings — say to the crayon scribbles all over the new wallpaper, and work quickly to find a solution (quite literally) that will help wipe the problem away.

Another helpful aspect of anger is that it doesn't last too long. Remember the comic book hero the Incredible Hulk who would swell into a green monster when he was angry, act out his rage on whatever vehicle, laboratory, or drug lord was in his way, then collapse exhausted and shrink back into his usual modest self?

The rapid transition out of the throws of anger is one reason that even when anger causes bad outcomes, they are usually not truly horrible. Anger just takes too much out of us to be maintained. Long-maintained anger is never as focused as the short-term variety, but it can lead to high stress levels, which have bad effects on our nervous, circulatory, and pulmonary systems.

So When Does it Start to Get Bad and Ugly?

An example of when your anger turns bad or ugly is when you would relate yourself to a sleeping lion. Everything is all right until something sets you off and you fly into a rage. This is when your anger becomes toxic because other people start to find it difficult to be around you. They always have to be on their guard, nervous and anxious, careful about the way they behave and the things they say because they don't want to send you into one of your rage episodes. Anger becomes toxic when it starts to poison almost every aspect of your life. It ruins your relationships. Other people don't feel safe being around you and you find that people often make excuses to avoid you. This is when anger turns from good to bad and ugly.

Ugly anger is the variety we see in the Incredible Hulk (before he collapses). It is often physically harming, aggressive, and violent, yet is still usually directed toward someone the aggressor knows. The worst of anger occurs when it is both violent and directed toward someone who cannot defend himself or herself. Aggressive and violent anger is often domestic, directed toward a partner, child, or elderly relative. It is criminal behavior.

Frequently, extreme anger is linked to other mental processes that are not operating optimally. If an angry parent is also drunk, then he or she may not have the ability to control the angry response as quickly when a child misbehaves. If he or she is angry and also mentally unstable, even due to a biochemical miswiring, such as General Anxiety Disorder or Chronic Depression, it can exacerbate angry impulses. Both alcohol and drugs (prescribed or recreational) can dull judgment and cause us to dismiss the inner voice that suggests it is time to calm down.

If we are angry and hungry, angry and ill, angry and tired, angry and feeling persecuted, angry and misled, angry and cold, angry and anxious, angry and out in the desert sun... any of these combinations can make it harder for us to allow our rational understanding of the situation at hand to take charge and quickly reset our response to something more appropriate for the situation.

Let's Evaluate How Angry You Really Are

While everyone gets angry, it is the *severity* of the anger and the way that it is managed that makes the difference between someone who experiences anger on a healthy spectrum and someone who has anger issues. Not everyone experiences anger to the same degree and that is also what makes the difference.

To start determining how angry you really are, you need first to be able to clearly identify and define what anger is. Anger is:

- An emotion which often either precedes or accompanies aggression
- An emotion that describes the way you feel towards your enemies or people you hate
- An emotion that makes you want to fight
- An emotion that makes you feel like you want to seek revenge
- An emotion that makes your blood boil
- An emotion you feel towards something you perceive as a "threat"
- An emotion that sets a negative precedent or tone
- An emotion that you feel brings out the worst in you
- An emotion that brings the aggressive side of your personality to the surface

Next, we need to identify how often you find yourself feeling angry. Start by answering the following questions:

- How often do you find yourself feeling angry? In the past week, for example, how many times did you find yourself feeling angry or irritated?
- What would your answer be in this instance?
    - I didn't feel angry at all
    - Maybe once or twice
    - Three to five times
    - Five times or more
    - I felt angry almost every day, several times a day

Anything that is more than three to five times a week means that you've got anger issues. But that's okay. The point is to be honest with yourself, even if you don't like the answer. Only then can you begin working to fix the problem.

Let's now assess your anger on a scale of one to 10.

- **Number 1** – Nothing really bothers you for long. You're happy, calm, and generally easy going. It takes a lot to set your anger off, and even then, it doesn't last for long.

- **Number 2** – You feel slight irritation and irritability from time to time, but it never lasts for very long. You usually get over it really quickly. Sometimes you do experience it on a higher scale, but it isn't enough to get you all worked up and distract you from what you should be doing.

- **Number 3** – You keep your anger on the inside and still respond negatively to people. Your anger and irritation are still not high enough to affect your decision making, but other people around you can start to tell that you are feeling annoyed.

- **Number 4** – You feel like you want to yell at someone who is in your way or telling someone off because you're feeling angry and irritable. You start to imagine scenarios in your mind where you are telling people off. You begin to contemplate actually acting on those feelings, but your anger is still not strong enough for you to take action just yet.

- **Number 5** – You start to feel angry at every little thing, and you may even feel angry at yourself. You can still control your reactions and your behavior, but it is now very obvious to everyone around you that you're feeling quite angry and irritable.

- **Number 6** – You start to feel like you could really tell someone off by this point and it is becoming harder to conceal your anger. You might bite someone's head off occasionally, but you are still making an effort to try and reign in your anger. It is getting harder though.

- **Number 7** – Anger is starting to affect you physically. Your muscles start to get tense, the vein in your temple starts to throb, and it feels like your blood is starting to boil. It is becoming harder to control your anger as you feel it creeping up to higher levels.

- **Number 8** – Your anger has now reached a point that you feel you want to do something about it. You want to yell at the person who is annoying you. You want to exact revenge on the person who wronged you. You start to feel a strong desire to inflict hurt or pain because you feel so angry. It is becoming harder to maintain a level head.

- **Number 9** – You've started acting on your angry impulses. You're yelling, shouting, telling people off, using verbal cues to let everyone know that you are *not* happy and telling them exactly what you think. Your anger is starting to rule you by this point, and you no longer care that your words may be hurting someone else's feelings.

- **Number 10** – By this point, you are now a danger to yourself and others around you. By this stage, you could resort to physical violence because you are so blinded by anger that you simply do not care anymore. Your anger has completely taken over, and you are no longer acting like yourself.

Where would you rate yourself on this scale in most situations? Where do you think you constantly hover around? This will give you a good indicator of how angry you really are most of the time. An emotionally healthy individual usually does not venture far from numbers 1 to 3. When anger becomes toxic is when you find yourself living in the 8 to 10 range all the time in almost every situation, even when it is not something serious.

Chapter 3: How to Find Control – Bad Anger, Long-Term Anger, and Explosive Temperament

Now that you know what causes anger, where it comes from, the good, the bad, and the ugly, it's time to get on to the important part – how to control that anger. Whether it be bad, long-term, or even the explosive temperament type of anger, the bottom line is that you want your anger kept in check, not just for your sake, but for everyone else around you too.

Anger can take on various forms. Some people feel angry but only for a brief moment and then they no longer dwell on it. Some people can't stop dwelling on anger, and it could take them hours, days, weeks, months, or even years to get over it. If they get over it at all, that is. Then, there are those who – when they do lose their temper – release their anger in what is known as explosive rage episodes.

No matter what form your anger may take, there is one thing that they all have in common – they are bad for your health and emotional state of being. Not only that, but harboring so much anger within you all the time can lead to risky, violent, and dangerous behavior patterns. It could further lead to problems like drug and alcohol abuse. Health-related problems as we have seen include coronary related heart disease. Other health problems which could result from severe anger issues include insomnia, headaches, muscular aches, and even digestive problems. Possibly the worst consequence, however, is the damage that it can do to your relationships, especially with the people who matter the most.

Tips to Start Learning How to Control Bad, Long-Term, and Explosive Anger

A common misconception about anger management is that it simply means you're learning how to *suppress* your anger. Suppressing your anger is not the goal. The goal here is to learn how to *control* that anger and to understand why you are reacting the way that you are. To learn how to respond better without jumping to anger as your first immediate reaction. To be able to walk away from situations which would have normally aggravated you without losing control. *That is the goal* of learning how to control your anger.

We do not want to get rid of anger entirely because remember that anger is part of the normal range of human emotions. To get rid of it entirely would be unnatural, and more importantly, you would lose out on the good benefits that healthy anger can do – which is why you need to learn *control* rather than suppression or elimination. The more you learn to control your anger, to express it in much healthier ways, the better it will be for your health, your happiness, and your relationships.

Start learning how to control your anger by:

- **Acknowledge your anger** – Denying your anger issues is one of the worst things you could do. More importantly, it will not help you learn to control it. Facing your problems may not be something that you want to do, but living in denial and ignoring it never solved anything either. If you do have anger issues you need to contend with, it is time to acknowledge them so you can actively do something about it. The more you deny your emotions and anger issues, the worst it will be for you when it comes to managing it. In fact, you may find yourself feeling angrier and losing your temper even more because you feel helpless and unable to control the situation.

- **Exploring the *reason* behind it** – Anger problems will always stem from something: your childhood, a previous traumatic experience, your role models growing up, or your stress levels. All these things add up and could build towards anger problems. To begin learning how to control your anger, you must first explore and connect with the *core reason* of anger. Your first line of response is how you control it. Anger is very often a response that is meant to cover-up other feelings which you may have. What are those feelings? Jealousy? Embarrassment? Hurt? Shame? Insecurity? These are the reasons you need to explore to know what your anger is covering up for you.

- **Changing the way that you think** – Don't expect other people to "accept" your anger because this is who you are and this is part of your personality. That is entirely the wrong approach to use. In fact, that is just you making excuses to justify your behavior without having to do anything to change it. You need to start changing the way that you think and realize that it is *your responsibility* to manage your anger issues. Other people should not have to tolerate or conform to your expectations. A social setting is not just about you; it is about everyone. Each person is equally important. Instead of expecting other people to conform to you, choose instead to *want to change to be better.* Think about how good it will feel to learn how to control your anger, for the people around you not to always be cautious and wary about when you're going to lose your cool next.

- **Practice deliberately slowing it down** – Emotions can get the best of you, especially anger, which is why learning to slow down your thoughts and emotions deliberately can go a long way towards helping you learn how to control your anger. Have you noticed how when you are starting to feel angry, your thoughts begin to race and get muddled up? Your breathing quickens, and suddenly it becomes difficult to keep a clear head, and you react based on your impulses instead? What you need to do now is to practice slowing your thoughts down to make sure that you are in control, not your anger, at every step of the way even when you're on the verge of getting angry. This can be achieved through practice. For example, what you could begin doing is when you next read something, read it slowly and deliberately focus on what you're reading. When you're writing something, focus on each word you're writing instead of going through the motions. This is how you practice being in control, by focusing on each thing that you are doing.

More Strategies that Can Be Used to Control Your Anger

What else can you do to get rid of this short fuse that you have? Changing your temperament is certainly not going to be an easy process, that's for sure. However, learning to control your anger can certainly be done with the help of the following techniques.

- **Learn to walk away** – If this is something you've never done before, now is a good time to start. This is going to require you to work hard to fight all your natural instincts to fight back at the situation or person that is making you angry. It is going to require you to swallow your pride and learn to walk away from a fight. It is time to wake up and realize that no amount of fighting and arguing is ever going to remedy all of a situation, so it is time to take the next best approach. By choosing to walk away until you've calmed down, instead of staying and fighting, you minimize the risk of having your anger escalate even further to a point you might do something you'll end up regretting. By disengaging yourself from the situation and allowing yourself some breathing space to calm your nerves, you're taking the mature approach in handling any person or situation. Responding in anger is never the solution, and you'll have a much better chance of a positive outcome if you choose this approach. Choose to walk away.

- **Distract yourself** – Anger can cause a lot of damage because it is such a disruptive emotion. All common sense just seems to go out the window in the heat of the moment. In Chapter 1, we talked about learning how to recognize the triggers that tend to set you off and cause your anger to escalate and this is why – because you need to distract yourself. When you recognize your triggers, it makes it easier to put a stop to it, to deflect your attention elsewhere until you've forgotten about what it was that was threatening your temper. You need to distance yourself from the triggers for as long as it takes until you are properly distracted enough that you forgot what it was you were about to feel angry about.

- **Let go of the need to always be right** – And to always have the last word. Why? Because it simply is not worth it. Anger occurs within a social context, and often arguments can go on forever if two people refuse to back down. Somebody always needs to have the last word, and this time it is *not going to be you*. By continuing to indulge in this behavior, you're not helping yourself or your anger issues. You are just making things much worse. Let go of the desire and the need to always be right. Yes, you're going to have to swallow your pride again and fight all your natural instincts to do so, but it will be worth it. It will get easier over time, and you'll feel a sense of satisfaction because, deep down, you know that it is the right thing to do. To put an end to anger or prevent it from escalating, somebody needs to make a move in the right direction. Why not you?

• **Use visualization** – Each time that you feel your anger is threatening to break through the surface, you need to stop immediately, close your eyes and start to visualize. It may sound silly, but it works. Visualization is an effective way to learn to relax, and it will help remind you of the goal that you need to accomplish. The goal here, in this case, would be learning how to control your anger. Picture peaceful scenes which will help you maintain a state of relaxed calm each time that you need it. This can be achieved with practice, and you will need to be able to vividly picture peaceful settings as though they were right in front of you. If the beach is a place you love that has been able to calm you down in the past, picture that. If it is a beautiful garden, picture that. Picture anything that infuses you with a sense of calm and even happiness if possible. This is a great distraction technique too. Being able to visualize and see your end goal will remind you of why you are doing what you are doing and help you to stay on course.

•**Exercising both mind and body** – This is the best outlet to channel all that anger and frustration that you are carrying around inside you. Exercising both your mind and body is a way of redirecting those feelings of anger towards a healthier release mechanism. Instead of taking your anger out on the people around you, channel it into your workouts. If you're doing kickboxing, for example, channel it into every punch and kick you make during the routine. If you're running, channel that energy out through every step that you take as your feet pound the pavement. Exercising both your mind and body simultaneously through yoga is another fantastic approach to take. Yoga is one of the best exercises you could encompass into your daily life because no other exercise medium combines both physical and mental training in one go. Yoga has been used for years as a way to strengthen both the mind and the body and is not just about getting rid of the energy that wears you down, but also building and strengthening yourself mentally, so it is better able to maintain control and keep your anger at bay.

• **Do something that makes you happy** – This is one of the oldest tricks in the book, yet it continues to remain one of the most effective. People who struggle with anger issues have a lot of misery and unhappiness inside them. How can you learn to control your anger if you're still harboring all that negativity inside you? There's nothing better at getting rid of all those unhappy, miserable feelings than very simply doing something that makes you happy. Indulge in a passion or a hobby. Throw yourself into an activity that you love. As much as anger and negativity can affect how you feel, it works the same way when you actively do something which makes you happy. With a happier state of mind, it makes it easier to think with a clearer head. You don't get as worked up so easily anymore, and it becomes much easier to learn how to control your anger issues. So, get out there and start doing all the things that you love again.

- **Breathe mindfully** – Mindful breathing is a useful exercise to have on hand because when faced with anger, you tend to lose control of your emotions. Whenever you're under stress and feeling angry, do you notice how your breathing becomes shallow and more tagged? By learning a few effective breathing techniques, you can dramatically control your response to a situation or a person. Mindful breathing is an exercise that takes practice, and it is something which is simple and easy to do right. You can practice this in your home or anywhere that you can find a quiet spot, and you should aim to practice this exercise often until you can see a difference in the way that you react to situations. Practice mindful breathing by sitting comfortably in a relaxed position, close your eyes, and focus on each breath that you take. Breathe deeply in and out, slow and steady, focusing on each inhale and exhale. Focus on the air that is flowing in and out of your body. Breathe in deeply through your nose and exhale slowly through your mouth. As you breathe in, count to five, pause, relax, and exhale while counting to five again. This repetitive exercise will help you relax, remain calm, and learn to be in control of your breathing patterns. Whenever you feel your anger rising, straight away change your focus to your breathing and begin mindfully breathing until you have successfully calmed yourself down again.

- **Keep a journal** – Journaling may not be for everyone, but when it comes to controlling your anger issues, it can be very therapeutic. More so than you may realize. One of the problems when it comes to anger is that you're so overwhelmed with all sorts of emotion (anger, frustration, irritation) that it all comes out all at once, especially when you have been keeping it bottled up for so long. Many people tend to strike or lash out in anger because they don't have proper channels or outlets to release that anger unto. This is where a journal comes in handy. Why would a journal help? Because a journal is something that is only for your eyes and it provides you with a safe and private place where you can express every feeling and emotion you have without the fear of being ridiculed or judged. More importantly, it is possibly *the safest* outlet for you to release your feelings of anger without hurting anyone or yourself in the process. Expressing your emotions in a journal will not cause problems or conflict with anyone because it is only for your eyes. Your journal is also a place where you can record the things that happened to you, and pour out all of your feelings of anger until you feel better.

A Few Other Good Tips to Keep in Mind

Because anger can be a difficult and challenging emotion to learn how to master and control, a few additional strategies come in handy. If you're finding it a challenge to change your thought patterns and the way that you react in anger, try the following strategies as reminders or affirmations that you can do this:

- I will not allow my anger to get the best of me. I am in control today and every day.
- I am capable of learning how to control my anger.
- I am in control of my thoughts and my reactions. I always have a choice to respond the right way.
- Anger is only temporary. Therefore, I will not let it get the best of me.
- I acknowledge that I am experiencing feelings of anger right now and I will do my best to calm myself down.
- I will not let my anger escalate out of control again. This is a challenge I can overcome.
- Every day I am getting better at controlling my anger. Every day I am stronger.
- I have more control over my emotions and reactions than I realize. I can do anything I set my mind to, and I choose to be in control.
- I want to get rid of anger issues so anger will not be a driving factor in my life anymore.

Chapter 4: Reexamining Angry Thoughts – How to Handle Long-Term Anger that Doesn't Go Away

Overcoming anger issues is a long journey. That is because there are so many aspects involved and so many challenges to overcome. Learning how to manage your anger is not just about learning how to handle your emotions and how to respond appropriately when you feel your anger rising. Anger management is also about *choosing what kind of person you want to be.* Do you want to become someone who is angry, resentful, bitter, and alone most of the time? Or do you want to become someone who is changing for the better? Someone with self-control, emotional intelligence, and the discipline needed to take control and manage your anger once and for all?

Let's start by reexamining your angry thoughts and why you have found it so hard to overcome long-term anger prior to this. Ask yourself the following questions:

- Have I identified the source of my anger?

- If I am currently feeling angry right now, why is that? What provoked this emotion? How long have I been feeling angry?

- Why am I finding it so difficult to let go of this anger?

Although you do have a right to experience anger (everyone does), you need to consider *why you find it hard to let go* of that anger? Is holding onto this anger for so long something that is justifiable? More importantly, is it worth wasting your precious time and energy being this angry all the time?

Overcoming long-term anger is something that only you can do. Nobody else can do it for you. If you're expecting someone else to apologize for being the cause of your anger, you will be waiting forever, especially if they have already forgotten about it and moved on. Now, it is up to you to do the same. Allow yourself time to be angry and express that anger appropriately, but learn to move on quickly.

To help you with this process, you can start by listing five ways that your life will be much better if you were to forget and let go of your long-term anger. That's a good place to start.

Other tools which you could use to help you reexamine your thoughts and learn to manage long-term anger include self-discipline, emotional intelligence, and neuro-linguistic programming, better known as NLP.

How Self-Discipline Helps Handle Long-Term Anger

The good news is this is *exactly* what you can do. To handle the long-term anger that you've been battling with for so long, not only do you have to reexamine your thoughts, but you need to *increase your self-discipline* too. Why do you need self-discipline to help you manage your anger? Because it is the answer you've been searching for. The key to *why* you haven't been able to manage your anger all this time.

Inside you, there is a power that you didn't know you had. The power to make the positive changes that you long to see in your life. To tap into that power, you need to have self-discipline. It helps you stay on track towards achieving your goals, towards reaching your full potential. In this case, the goal here is how to manage and handle the long-term anger within you that you've been struggling to conquer all this time.

Self-discipline and self-control are two traits which are not that far apart. The reason that they can help you learn how to manage your anger is that these two qualities help you with the ability to control your impulses, emotions, and behaviors. This ability is also sometimes referred to as willpower, and it is a quality that has helped drive many people towards success. This will now be your key to successfully learning how to manage and control your long-term anger. Everyone can learn how to build a healthy self-discipline habit. It is simply up to you whether you choose to do it or not. Once you do, you will be amazed at what a tremendous impact it will have on your life and your attempts at learning how to manage your anger. You will see what difference it can make.

Self-discipline is such an important skill set to possess. Among the benefits that this trait brings includes:

- Helping you stick to the decisions that you make, to keep on going when the going gets tough.

- It gives you the extra push and the drive that you need to smash through obstacles.

- It helps you with self-control, making it less likely that you're going to give in to your desires and temptations. In this case, self-control helps you manage your anger.

- It helps stop you from reacting impulsively based on your emotions, which are what you need if you hope to control your anger.

- It helps you to stay focused on what you're doing.

Anger is often a self-control issue. You are unable to control your impulses and your responses because you don't have the willpower and the discipline (yet) to get a handle on your anger before it rises to the surface and erupts. Learning how to control your anger is something that has to start *inside* of you, and it needs to start with self-control and self-discipline. You have the power within you to tell yourself:

- I *WILL NOT* lose my temper
- I *WILL NOT* explode
- I *WILL NOT* hold onto my anger any longer
- I *WILL NOT* let my anger rob me of any more joy

This is not stopping your anger, but rather, it is you *declaring what you are going to do*. That is self-control and self-discipline. It helps you take charge and take the control away from your anger.

To begin building habits that will improve your self-control and self-discipline, use the following strategies:

- **Get rid of excuses NOW** – There is no more room for excuses if you're going to learn how to manage your long-term anger. When you're reexamining your thoughts, ask yourself how often you make excuses to justify your behavior? Too often? Then it needs to stop right now. It is time to kick those excuses out the door and into the bin where they belong. Self-discipline leaves no room for excuses – only action.

- **Make a list & write it down** – Make a list of all the changes that you want to see happen so that it is clear as day right in front of you. Making a list is one of the most underestimated tools around, and it cannot be stressed enough just how useful it can be. As human beings, we are very visual creatures. Something becomes more believable when we can see it in front of our eyes. So write down your goals and what you hope to achieve in learning how to manage your anger, and each time you feel your willpower waning, whip out the list and take a good, hard look at it again.

- **Be persistent** – This is such an important quality to have as you work on improving your self-control and self-discipline. It can be so easy to give up when things get tough, but persistence is living proof that you have it within you to achieve anything that you set your mind to. When you persist through one weakness and overcome it, you feel a sense of accomplishment, which will be one of the most rewarding feelings you will ever experience. Persistence makes you appreciate every accomplishment and makes every victory taste just a little bit sweeter. It shows you that you are capable of anything that you set your mind to. Each time you push through a challenge with persistence, you emerge stronger, victorious, and better than when you first started. This is what you need on your side as you begin working on improving your self-discipline.

- **Know what you want** – You can't find the motivation and the drive that you need if you don't know what you want. In this case, you need to tell yourself that you *want* to learn how to manage your long-term anger issues. Ask yourself why you want to achieve this so badly? What is the purpose of you doing all of this? You must be able to specifically answer each question with conviction and belief. That is how you build up the self-discipline that you need to learn how to manage your anger – by remembering *why* you're doing this and *what* you want to accomplish at the end of this journey.

- **Prep yourself mentally** – Your mind is your most powerful tool, and this is going to be the key to increasing your self-discipline levels. Prepare yourself mentally by using positive affirmations, listening to motivational podcasts, reading inspirational books, whatever it takes to prepare you with a positive mindset that will help you stick to this course of action and see it through.

If you're not disciplined enough to put in the work and the effort, you're never going to accomplish the results that you want and learn to master your long-term anger.

How to Manage Long-Term Anger with Emotional Intelligence

Emotional intelligence can be a wonderful tool in helping you manage your long-term anger and reexamine your angry thoughts because of the five components that emotional intelligence is made of. The five core principles include having self-awareness, self-regulation, empathy, social skills, and motivation. These five principles are essential to learning how to manage your anger and reexamine your thoughts because it forces you to stop and reflect, to see beyond your anger.

Self-awareness allows you to view your emotions from an objective standpoint, to take a step back and reflect on why you're feeling such a strong emotion, which in this case is anger. It allows you to make the connection between your heart and your head so that your reactions are not ruled entirely by your emotions (heart). This is how you begin reexamining your angry thoughts – by using self-awareness to reflect upon why you feel this way and use the thinking part to assess what needs to be done about it. Self-regulation, on the other hand, helps you *control* your responses, to stop you from reacting impulsively from a place of anger. It works together with self-awareness and by being fully aware of your anger, its triggers and its causes, it puts you in a much better position to determine what you need to do and what the best approach would be by regulating your behavior when you're angry.

Another emotional intelligence trait which will help you reexamine your angry thoughts is empathy. This is the ability to put yourself in the other person's shoes to understand where they are coming from. It is not just about your anger and the way that you are feeling; it is also about them. If you are feeling angry, what about them? If they are feeling that way, then *why?* And is it for the same reasons you are? Using empathy and social skills in tandem will help you better work through the problems that are causing your anger to rise because, for all you know, the other person you're having a conversation with could be on the same page as you are. It is through empathy and social skills that you will come to an understanding. Combine that with the motivation and determination to *want* to learn how to control your anger, and you will have a much better chance of amicably resolving the argument, without anyone having to have their feelings hurt.

How to Manage Long-Term Anger with Neuro-Linguistic Programming (NLP)

NLP is a concept that focuses on the language that your mind speaks. It is about understanding what your brain is trying to tell you. Without this understanding, it would be challenging to connect yourself to your thoughts, which would then make it more difficult for you to reexamine your angry thoughts. You need NLP to help you connect with your mind and understand your thoughts in a way you have never been able to before. This is how you will learn to manage your long-term anger.

In moments of anger where your emotions rule the situation, NLP is how you will take control again. This concept can help you make a deeper connection between why you are holding onto your anger for so long and open you up to new ideas and possibilities to be more in tune with what's happening internally. To manage your long-term anger issues, you must be able to identify your current limitations and break through them.

NLP's primary concept is about learning how to tap into the unconscious part of your mind and become more adept at managing your emotions. It helps you learn how to manage the situation according to the circumstances you're in, which will help you empathize on a deeper level and maybe see things from a whole new perspective. Suddenly, what was making you so angry may not seem so important anymore, but you won't realize that until your mind and your emotions can make a steady, strong connection to one another.

There are several concepts in NLP which can help you manage your long-term anger issues, one of which is called the Perceptual Positions technique. This NLP strategy teaches you to see things from the other person's perspective which also helps to build up your empathy skills and social skills in the process. With greater levels of empathy, you will develop a better understanding of the people around you which will give you something else to focus on other than your anger. This, in turn, will allow you to see that there are more important things than anger to think about, which will hopefully make it easier for you to let go of any anger you've been holding onto all this time.

And when it comes to reexamining your thoughts, NLP's Content Reframing technique is an excellent strategy whenever you feel that all you can focus on is the negative. Reexamining your thoughts means you need to reframe the way that you think about them. Instead of just seeing them as thoughts which are fueling your anger, *reframe* them into something that empowers you by changing the meaning that you've been associating that thought with all this time. Instead of seeing it as a thought that is causing you anger, see it as a learning lesson instead, an experience which taught you something new. By reframing the way that you think about your angry thoughts, you will be able to see things from an entirely different perspective, and with new focus points to think about, you'll realize that maybe what was making you so angry was not really that big of a deal after all.

Expressing Your Anger in Healthy Ways with Communication Skills

Good communication skills require two things: that you be an active, good listener and you see things from the other person's point of view (like empathy). Empathy is a skill that we all lack when we are angry, just like it was highlighted in the emotional intelligence section above – which is why something else you can learn to do to manage your long-term anger is to learn how to communicate effectively.

Expressing your anger effectively through communication skills is not so much about what you say but *how* you say it. The louder you speak, the less you will make yourself heard. Think about it, would you listen to someone who was yelling at you? Shouting right in front of your face? Definitely not – you would shut down immediately and completely block out what the person is trying to say.

The thing is, when you're busy yelling your head off in anger, you don't realize that the message you are trying to convey gets lost in translation. If you want to be heard, you need to work on your volume and the speed at which you speak. The angrier you are, the faster and louder you tend to speak. However, these two aspects are what you need to start working on if you want to avoid irritating the person you're talking to and having the discussion escalated into a full-blown argument. You start speaking a lot faster when you're angry too. Do you notice that? It is as if you can't wait to get your anger out quick enough. Stop, pause, and pace yourself if you want to make yourself heard.

Other strategies you could use to still communicate effectively while managing your anger at the same time include the following:

- **Keeping it short and concise** – As angry as you are, you need to make an effort to keep the conversation short and concise. It makes it easier for the person on the other end of the conversation to follow your thought process and listen to what it is you're trying to say. This helps to prevent long, drawn-out arguments too which only end up with more hurtful words being exchanged on both ends. You may be angry, but remember that lashing out at the other person is not going to do anybody any favors. Avoid long and unnecessarily elaborate explanations to keep the conversation effective and assertive. This way, you get your point across and say what it is you want to say while still sticking to the facts and key points. This is how you effectively handle a conversation in anger.

- **Highlight your empathy** – Imagine that you're in a heated argument. You're angry, and you're trying to let the other person know *why* you're upset. When that person responds with, "I hear what you're saying, and I can see where you're coming from," doesn't that make you feel so much better? Expressing empathy is how you can effectively handle an angry conversation and keep it from escalating any further. Long-term anger is often a result of feelings of dissatisfaction, feeling like you still have not said your piece, and there's more you would like to get off your chest. You feel like the other person still doesn't "get it". This could contribute to you being unable to let go of your anger and holding onto it for a long time. The next time you're in a heated argument, try expressing your empathy and see what difference it can make to the situation.

• **Manage your tone of voice** – To effectively communicate in an angry argument, you will need to exercise a lot of self-control on your part. This will allow you to remain assertive yet calm enough not to start yelling and be blinded by anger. Self-control is going to come into play with the way that you manage your tone of voice to make sure that your volume is not escalating with every sentence that you speak. A challenging exercise to master in the beginning but it can be done with patience and practice.

• **Under no circumstance should you be forceful** – Do not force the person you're in conversation with to go along with your way of thinking. That is not being an effective communicator; that's on the verge of bullying. You'll be crossing that fine line and venturing into angry aggression. You can still get your point across while communicating effectively during a heated conversation by still choosing to be respectful towards the people you're speaking to. Acknowledge and respect that you have no control over what other people think or the way they behave, and the best thing you could do for yourself and everyone else is to be firm with your own decision, but still remain calm and respectful even though you may be feeling angry. That is how you effectively manage your long-term anger and keep it from becoming an explosive rage episode.

Chapter 5: Methods for Dealing with Anger – Relaxation Techniques, Letting Go, and Forgiveness

If only staying calm and collected was as easy as losing our tempers! The world would certainly be a much better place, wouldn't it? Getting angry can certainly make your blood boil and your blood pressure rise, which is why it is important to learn how to relax and calm your nerves before things spiral out of control. High blood pressure is a condition that is for life, and once that happens, you're looking at a lifetime of medication just trying to keep it under control. Is your anger worth risking your health like that? No, it most certainly is not.

Learning to Relax and Keep Your Cool – Effective Relaxation Techniques to Help You Calm Down

Relaxation techniques are going to be the best thing for you when it comes to dealing with your anger. This helps prevent you from getting out of control and doing something that you will regret later on. If this has happened far too often than you'd like to admit, perhaps it is time to start adopting these relaxation techniques to help you calm down.

Relaxation Technique #1 – Exercise

One of the best relaxation techniques that can do wonders to improve your health overall is exercise. And it doesn't cost you a thing (unless you join a gym or classes of course). Whether you realize it or not, your lifestyle habits play a big part in the current state of your health. If you're dealing with anger issues, it is likely you've already experienced firsthand some of the effects that anger can do to you. Internal factors such as high levels of stress daily, emotional issues and problems, feeling unhappy and worked up are also factors that can contribute and eventually lead to high blood pressure over a prolonged period. All of this is related to anger, which is why it can cause a lot of the heart-related diseases that we talked about in the previous chapters.

This is why, as part of your relaxation process, one technique you should turn to is exercise. Exercise is good for you. Exercise helps not only to elevate your mood but as your body gets fitter and stronger, your energy levels will increase, and you'll find you're able to accomplish so much more in a day. Exercising also helps to boost your endorphin levels, the hormone which helps you feel good and feel happy. If you're holding onto a lot of anger issues, this is certainly something that you are going to need. Exercising is a channel, an outlet for you to let out any frustration or stress you may have so that it isn't bottled up inside you. Just speak to anyone who works out regularly, and they will be able to attest to how much better they feel after they've done a workout. Exercise is an excellent relaxation technique that can help teach you how to manage your stress and how to release and let go of any current stress you may be carrying around with you. The next time you feel angry and worked up, try doing some exercise. Notice a difference in how you feel?

Relaxation Technique #2 – Yoga

Yoga is another great method of relaxation whenever you're feeling stressed and angry. Why is it so great at helping you relax? Because it focuses on slow, controlled movements. It doesn't put much strain or stress on your body's muscles but instead focuses on building strength through controlled movements. Yoga centers mainly on three main principles to help you achieve a state of calm: meditation, deep breathing techniques, and controlled physical activity.

Meditation teaches you how to breathe deeply and mindfully, drawing more oxygen into your body which helps your blood flow better. It gives you something to focus on other than what is making you angry. Deep breathing teaches your mind and body to relax, opens your muscles, and slowly releases the stress from your body with each deep breath in and out that you take. It focuses on balancing, energizing, and awakening your mind, body, and soul.

One such movement or pose in yoga known as the *Asana pose* is a good technique to adopt because it is designed to help your body achieve peace and focus through a series of movements and stretches. The movements are steady and comfortable for your body, encouraging you to be relaxed yet firm during the movement. The movements in this pose will help you greatly reduce your stress and anger levels, and it is something that you should turn to whenever you feel like you might need some calm amidst the chaotic anger in your life.

Relaxation Technique #3 – Meditation

Meditation is an experience that is truly life-changing, which in the case of learning how to manage your anger is something that you are going to need. This practice has survived for thousands of years for one very simple reason – it is *effective*. Meditation teaches you to be mindful of everything that is going on around you, to be present, and in tune with what is happening around you at this moment. Just like the other relaxation techniques above, it gives you something to focus on other than your anger. It helps you focus on the here and the now, not on what happened previously or what may happen in the near future.

Learning to meditate to relieve stress is one of the best things you can do for yourself when it comes to learning how to manage your anger and calm down. If you are a beginner to this process, opt for a guided meditation to help you transition into this practice. Guided meditation is a practice that everyone, no matter what their age, can adapt and you will find it extremely useful if you are a first-time practitioner because of the guided cues to help you along the process.

You owe it to yourself to spend a few minutes a day, every day, to start taking care of your mind, body, and soul. You've wasted so much of your energy on anger that has brought nothing beneficial to your life. It is now time that you start taking care of your body while learning effective techniques to manage your anger in the process. Meditation has proven time and time again to be one of the best tools around today to help you conquer stress and anger, and because it is so effective, this is one technique you want to keep close at hand.

Learning to Forgive

Forgiving someone who wronged you is never an easy process. In fact, for those with severe anger issues, who are capable of holding a grudge for years, this is like asking them to do the impossible. It is much easier to hold onto a grudge than it is to forgive. That's why they call forgiveness the act of *being the bigger person.* It takes great inner strength to truly forgive wholeheartedly without expecting anything in return.

Getting angry is easy. With just a snap of your fingers, you can immediately get angry. But forgiveness? That's going to take much more work. It is a skill which you must learn, similar to riding a bicycle, learning to read and write, playing the piano, or playing a sport. It is a skill that everyone has to learn because very rarely are people born with the ability to forgive as quickly as they can get angry.

One way of learning forgiveness is when you were growing up. You witnessed members of your family forgiving each other or your parents displaying acts of forgiveness. If you experienced this growing up, forgiveness might be a slightly easier task for you.

Forgiveness is something that is going to take time. It isn't going to happen overnight. That's one thing that you need to be clear about right from the beginning. Like everything else, it is a journey and the time it takes for you to reach your destination would depend entirely on your personality and how quickly you learn to adapt. The longer you hold onto a grudge or your anger, the longer the journey will be.

This part of the process will also require that you have support on your side. Because it can be so difficult and it is a process which requires great strength and courage, and even maturity on your part, the more support you have around you, the higher your chances of success will be. Do you already have a role model who is an exemplary beacon of forgiveness? Look to them for inspiration. Learn as much as you can from them, the way they forgive, and what they do to move past their anger. Tell your family and friends about what you're trying to do and let them know you would appreciate their support along the way.

Forgiveness is something that no one can force you to do. It is a choice that you alone must make. When you do choose to forgive, you must do so without expecting anything in return. Do it for your own peace of mind, not because you feel forced into it. Everything about this anger management process is about helping you regain your happiness once more and to not let anger rob you of any more joy or energy than it already has, including learning to forgive others. Do it because it is going to make things better for you and you alone.

It is also going to be a process which demands some sacrifice from you. What you would be sacrificing is:

- Your pride
- Your belief that things should always be fair to you
- Your belief that you are the victim in the situation
- Your belief that you are using your anger as a shield to protect you from even more pain
- Thinking that the other person owes you an apology before you can even consider forgiving them
- Giving up wanting revenge
- The feeling of entitlement that the other person owes you something after causing you pain and anger
- Your belief that forgiving is a sign of weakness on your part

People make mistakes. That is human nature. We hurt other people's feelings whether we intend to or not. Even you have been guilty of hurting someone else, and if they managed to forgive you, you can do the same. It is your pride and your ego that is currently standing in the way of you being able to forgive someone. However, ask yourself this: is it really worth it to be holding onto your anger? Whom is it hurting in the end?

The types of support that you can seek out, so you learn to become more forgiving, include the following:

- **Familial support** – Family is the best place to begin. Nobody will be there by your side through good times and bad the way family is. They can be your pillars of strength and provide you with the emotional support that you need when you find yourself really struggling to forgive.

- **Getting enough information** – When you've got all the information that you need, it could be of great help during the forgiveness process. Maybe you're feeling angry at a friend over an argument that you had, but you didn't realize that prior to the argument, that friend had just undergone something very stressful or something that caused them a great deal of unhappiness. Knowing the information that you didn't know makes it easier to forgive if you can empathize with them.

- **Honest feedback support** – You need people on your side who will be willing to provide you with honest feedback even at the risk of triggering your anger. This will serve as a good test for how well you're doing in terms of managing your anger when you can receive honest, constructive criticism without feeling defensive or immediately becoming angry. Honest feedback will give you a good idea of your progress, the strides you have made, and what else you need to do to improve.

Other Methods You Can Use to Help You Manage Your Anger

You always have a choice when it comes to anger. It is easy to forget that when you're so consumed by that emotion, but you do. You choose whether you want to respond or react. You choose how long you decide to hold onto your anger. You choose how much of that anger you let affect your life.

Some questions for you to ponder on include:

- Do you want to be this angry, emotional, and uncontrollable person for the rest of your life?

- Do you always want to let your emotions rule the day?

- Do you want to continue spending the rest of your life constantly apologizing for your actions and poor judgment?

- Do you want to spend the rest of your life trying to fix relationships which you damaged out of anger?

- Do you want to be judged by others? To be viewed as someone they should "stay away from" because of your bad temper?

Clearly, the answer is going to be *no*, which is why you've decided to pick up this book and find out what you can do to manage your anger in the first place. You're ready to make the necessary steps towards positive change, and that's a fantastic start!

It is now time to break your lifelong angry habits, so don't feel discouraged if you find this part of the process difficult. You've spent your entire life up until this point only knowing one way to deal and respond to your anger. Change is going to take some adjusting and getting used to, but it can be done. Now that you know the most effective relaxation techniques and that learning to forgive is part of the process, here are some other things you can do to help you manage your anger.

- **Avoid other angry people** – This one is a given. It works along the same lines as staying away from negative or toxic people if you want to achieve success in your life. If you want to learn how to become a better, less angry person, you need to stay far away from other angry people. Even if they may be your friends, this is something that must be done. If you don't keep a distance from them, they could significantly set you back in your efforts to control your anger. As much as we like to think we are strong, negative behavior patterns have a way of rubbing off on us despite our best efforts. You need to do yourself a favor and stay away from other angry people.

- **Practice patience** – This one is tricky as many angry people tend to be impatient and impulsive. You're going to have to fight all your natural instincts here and learn to exercise patience. It's not going to be easy in the beginning, but it can be done. Remind yourself that the situation you are in is not going to last forever. It isn't going to stick around and make you angry. It will come to pass, and all you have to do on your part is be patient and wait for it to fade away. Patience is not a concept that is designed to make things worse for you. Patience is a virtue. It pays to be patient, especially in anger as it can save you from many situations you might regret later.

- **By just being quiet** – When you're in an angry confrontation, the more you say, the worse things become. Once something has been said, it can never be undone, and in some cases, no amount of apologizing will be enough to remedy the situation. Why not try the opposite approach and choose to be quiet instead? Understandably, it is going to take a lot of willpower on your part, but it is much, much better than digging yourself into an even deeper hole just to satisfy the urge to say something. Whenever you're angry, put up a good fight with yourself and choose to remain quiet instead. Go off into a quiet corner or space where you can be by yourself until you have relaxed enough to come back to the situation again. It will save you much regrettable behavior in the long run.

- **Find something that makes you laugh** – Laughter truly is the best remedy for just about any situation. Whenever you feel that you need to calm down and manage your anger, find something or do something that makes you laugh. Listen to a funny story, read a joke, watch something that makes you burst with laughter and lighten your mood. Nothing cures anger faster than just having a good, hearty laugh.

Chapter 6: There Must Be Another Way – How to Solve Problems Without Anger

If you're thinking that there must be another way to solve problems without falling back on anger, you're right. There is. However, it is first going to require you to change your mindset and the way that you've been viewing the world all this time.

Angry people tend to have a very negative, pessimistic, and narrow-minded view of the world. All they see are the problems and the reasons for them to get angry. They can't see the good that is in front of them because of how their mindset is currently functioning. What you need to do right now to initiate change is to *change the way that you think.* Is it possible to change our mindset?

It is, and more importantly, it is necessary if you are ever going to see real change happening in your life. Especially if you hope to learn to control your anger issues. Our mindsets here refer to the beliefs that we have about ourselves and the qualities we possess. Some people can better control their anger than others because they have *cultivated* their mindset to become this way. People are unique individuals, and no two people are going to think, behave, or act in the same way. The difference in backgrounds, life experiences, beliefs, and situations all contribute to the kind of mindset that you have right now. If all you have been exposed to are negative mindsets, then this is all that you are going to know. It contributes to why you are an angry person.

Those who have learned to control their anger didn't manage it because they are less angry individuals. Anger is an emotion that everyone experiences – even children. The difference lies in how we each choose to respond to the anger that we experience. Steve Maraboli, the author of *The Power of One,* said that every day is a new day and it is up to you how you shape it. This statement concisely points out how much of a difference having the right mindset can have. No matter what may be happening or what situations you may be facing, it is the way that you perceive things which will make the difference. If you constantly perceive everything as situations which are only going to aggravate your anger, then that will eventually become your reality. If you believe that it is possible not to let your anger get the best of you, that it is completely possible to resolve problems without needing anger, then that will become your reality.

Our thoughts can hurt us more than we know. The problem with a negative and angry mindset is that it acts like an anchor that weighs you down, and while it may be hard to overcome, it is not impossible. To start working on improving your mindset, so you can learn how to control your anger better, here is what you need to do:

- **Believe in yourself** – If you don't believe that you are capable of change, who else will? You'll never truly achieve the level of positive mindset you hope for if you still have those nagging thoughts at the back of your mind that make you doubt if you can even pull this off. You'll never be able to become the true master of your temper if you don't first *believe that you can do it*. By believing you can achieve it, you've already put yourself one step closer to making it happen for real.

- **Be someone who is flexible** – Whenever you're angry, you can feel an overwhelmingly strong desire to want to control the situation to your advantage. You're not thinking about the other person anymore because when you're angry, it becomes all about you. Unfortunately, the reality is that you cannot always have full control and the sooner you can accept that, the faster it will be for you to build a better, healthier, and more importantly, positive frame of mind. It is time to learn to be flexible and let go, to understand that while there may be some things which are beyond your control, one thing you do have control over is how *not to respond in anger*.

- **Keep only positive people in your circle** – Stay away from the rageaholics but keep the ones who radiate with positivity close to you. This is how to learn to see things from a better perspective, to improve your mindset by emulating those who have already done it. Negative and angry people will only weigh you down just like anchors. Even worse, they will rub off on you and make it impossible to get your anger management under control. When you surround yourself with only people with positive mindsets, you'll slowly adapt the way you think to emulate them as their wisdom, their outlook, stories, and affirmations slowly seep into your way of thinking.

- **Build up your resilience** – Having a better mindset will involve you working on building up your resilience. This means that you will have to become a more determined individual, no longer let challenges and setbacks affect you mentally and emotionally, and keep persisting even when things are difficult. Building up your resilience until you are a stronger person mentally and emotionally will help you control your anger in a way that you were never able to before.

- **Get a mantra** – It's not different from having positive affirmations. Having a personal mantra is something that will empower you and remind you to be optimistic each time you find yourself face-to-face with another challenge. A mantra like *I am the one in control, not my anger* or *I will not let my anger get the best of me today!* is good enough to start. A mantra can be anything that you want. It is entirely up to you. All you have to do is pick one that makes you feel empowered enough to change your mindset. Repeat it over and over again until you find your mindset shifting in the direction that you want it to go.

- **The mirror technique** – This technique is a great one for exercising change for your mindset. Whenever you look at your reflection in the mirror each morning, say something positive. Tell yourself, for example, *I am not someone who is ruled by anger.* Be genuine and believe every word that you say. Say each word with conviction while you look yourself in the eye. You could also repeat your mantra this way. Keep up this habit, and soon it will become an effortless exercise as your mindset improves.

You Also Need to Understand Your Anger

You need to understand your anger before you can learn to manage it. How would you manage something that you don't fully understand? Which is why it is so important to analyze the feelings that you have, dissect them and get to the root of the problem, and ask yourself how you could respond better in the situation.

Here are a couple of crucial questions that you need to start thinking about in times of anger:

- **Who am I angry at? Really?** – Although your first instinct may be to immediately point the finger at the person who provoked your anger, pause for a moment and look a little deeper. Is this really the case? Or were you already carrying around pent-up anger that you may not have realized and the person just happened to say or do something that triggered it? It is easy to immediately point the blame at whatever seems to be the most convenient, but if you want to learn how to solve problems without anger, you need to start looking a little deeper. Things may not always be what they seem.

- **Is this the right time or place to get angry?** – There is a time, and a place, for everything, including managing your moments of anger. For example, having an explosive episode right in the middle of your office in front of your boss or manager is not the right time or place. Letting your temper fly in the middle of the supermarket aisle is not the right time or place. The thing about anger is it can sometimes crop up at the most inconvenient of times. To learn how to start solving problems without anger, always stop and ask yourself, *Is this the right time or place to get angry*? If you know it is inappropriate, then don't do it.

- **Exactly *why* am I angry?** – You may have been angry for so long that it seems like second nature to you. You don't even know *why* you're angry anymore. Think of a time where you argued with a friend or family member, and the two of you ended up not speaking for years. The problem seems to have faded away as you went about your daily lives. When someone asks what happened between the two of you, you find yourself lost for words because you can't exactly remember why you were so angry in the first place or what the argument was even about. That happens when you let your anger drag on for so long. You've forgotten what the underlying issue really was. There is always a better way to resolve problems without having to resort to anger, but it first requires that you *understand why on earth* you were so angry in the first place? If it wasn't worth it, then why do it?

- **Is the consequence worth it?** – For every action, there is an equal and opposite reaction. This is Newton's infamous third law of physics, and it's very applicable to moments of anger. Everything that you do in anger has a price and a consequence which follows. Each time you feel yourself about to fly off the handle, you need to stop and ask yourself if the price you have to pay for this brief moment of satisfaction is going to be worth it. Is it worth ruining relationships? Is it worth causing even bigger problems later on? Is it worth damaging your reputation over? Is it worth wasting your energy on? Don't forget that things said in anger can never be unsaid. Once it's out there, there's no taking it back. The moment you say something hurtful in anger, that you wish you could take back, is the moment that it may be too late.

Now, What are My Options to Resolve Problems Without Anger

It is always up to you to choose how you would like to respond. There is no hard and fast rule that the only acceptable response to situations which incite you is anger. Anger, in fact, should be a last resort, even better if you don't have to resort to anger at all. The question is, *how do you want to resolve the problem?* You have an infinite number of options depending on the time, place, circumstance, and the present situation. However, at the end of the day, the choice remains yours.

Some strategies to keep in mind on how to resolve problems without having to resort to anger are:

- **Forget about exercise** – Exercising your right to be angry that is. You may feel that you are entitled to that moment of anger because this person or situation has wronged you, but that is exactly how *not* to keep your anger under control. Want to resolve problems without resorting to anger? Forget about your right to be angry.

- **Learn to listen actively** – If you're in an argument with someone, learn to listen actively to what it is they're saying. Listening and listening actively are two different things. The latter will help you to empathize more with the person you're in an argument with and see where they are coming from. This, in turn, will help to minimize the possibility of the argument escalating to the point that you will both regret later on. Listening actively means being mindful of everything the other person is saying. You're making a conscious effort to actively receive and process the information that is being given to you, and you're able to connect with what's being said, reflect on the information, and finally be able to provide constructive, thoughtful and proactive responses because of it. By listening actively, you will see that every problem can be resolved amicably and there is no real reason to bring anger into the mix at all.

- **Always check in with your emotions** – This is where being mindful again comes into play. No matter what situation you find yourself in, always remember to stop and check in with yourself. How are you feeling? Are you all right? How does this person or situation make you feel right now? If you feel yourself getting irritated or stressed, what can you do about it? Close your eyes and take a couple of measured deep breaths, remind yourself to focus on your present, and shift your mind away from what is threatening to trigger your anger. Remind yourself that you *want to resolve problems without the need for anger*.

- **You don't need the last word** – Resist the urge to have the final say. It is not always about you. The constant need to be right, to always have the last word just to quench your satisfaction and ego is exactly how anger makes problems and arguments much worse. If you want to resolve problems without having to resort to anger, learn to swallow your pride and resist the urge to fight back. Resist the urge to counter what someone else is saying with another defensive argument of your own. That does nothing to help the situation.

- **Talk about your feelings** – Before you begin to get angry, try talking about your feelings beforehand. If you know you are about to have an unpleasant conversation with someone, start by saying, "I know we need to talk about this and this is the way I'm feeling right now." Explain your position in a calm, controlled manner in a neutral tone of voice that does not imply you are blaming or accusing the other person of anything. Being able to verbalize your feelings instead of jumping headfirst into the situation is how you keep anger out of the equation. By talking about your feelings beforehand, the other person will right away be able to see where you are coming from and how you already feel before the discussion.

- **No judgments please** – If you go into a conversation with an already preconceived notion in mind or even prejudice, that is just an argument waiting to happen. Although yes, admittedly, we have all been guilty of being critical or judgmental. This is not the best approach to use if you are hoping to resolve problems without anger. You need to leave your judgments and criticism at the door where they belong and don't bring them into the conversation or situation you may currently be engaged in. Being overly critical is how you put yourself at risk of making potentially snarky or sarcastic comments which could aggravate the situation and cause an argument. That is how you learn how to resolve problems without the need for anger.

- **No more blame** – It is time to stop the blame game once and for all. If you're always looking for an opportunity to blame someone else, to eagerly shift the blame, so you end up looking like "the good one", how do you ever hope to resolve conflict without having to resort to anger? Always looking for a chance to blame someone else is a sign of someone with low emotional intelligence, an individual who is toxic and difficult to be around. Don't be this person because you know you are capable of being so much better than that. Enough with the blame game; it is time to toss that aside and start focusing on resolving problems like a mature individual.

- **Ditch the negative mindset** – A negative mind will be able to see nothing but problems in front of them. It is almost like negativity somehow blinds you to the opportunities and the other options which are in front of you. There could be a dozen other pathways which you could take to avoid anger in that situation, but if you're always harping on the negative, you won't be able to see any of those things. All you would be able to think about is how bad and how unfair everything is, or how angry this person is making you right now.

Chapter 7: Avoid & Escape – Catching Anger Before It Hits at Home, Work and Public Arenas

At home. At work. In a public arena.

These are the three main areas where you should strive to focus on managing your temper the most. Home and work especially are the two main areas that you are going to spend the most time every day. When you're not at home, you're at work. When you're not at work, you're often at home or in a public area. Therefore, it is only fitting that you put your best effort forward when it comes to managing your anger within these three areas.

What you want to do right now is to try and avoid and keep your anger from surfacing altogether by catching that emotion and doing something about it before it starts to take over. You are trying to be the one in control right now.

Catching Anger Before It Hits at Home

Your home is where you feel comfortable, free to be yourself. It's your safe space and your sanctuary. Which is why sometimes we don't even think twice about trying to control our anger when we're in our homes; we just let it fly. Only later do we realize that maybe we shouldn't have done that. We're not as controlled as we are at home around family because we assume that they already know this is who we are and they have to accept it whether they like it or not. Because they're family.

However, this is not the right way to think at all. Just because they are your family, it doesn't mean they are without feelings. They can get just as hurt by your words and actions as strangers or friends do. Just because they are family, it doesn't automatically mean they have to put up with everything and not feel any pain when you hurt them or that saying sorry is going to make everything okay, like nothing happened.

Family is the very reason *why* you should try so hard to control and manage your anger. These are people that you love, people who mean more to you than anyone else in the world. They are the people who are worth fighting for, and you should put up a good fight against your anger, starting in your home.

To start catching anger in your home before it gets out of control, here is what you can start doing:

- **Always choose to respond kindly** – It can be easy to lash back when a family member confronts you angrily or does something that aggravates you enough to the point of anger. For example, teenagers drive their parents crazy with their attitude at times and when that happens, what do the parents do? Automatically the parents will jump into the argument because they are feeling annoyed already and if the situation continues, both parties could end up in a heated argument with each other. What should you do in a situation like this? Always choose to be kind and empathize. Remember that this is a person you love and getting angry is simply not worth the time, energy, and effort. There are always other ways to resolve conflict which don't have to involve arguments all the time. Let love be the reason that you choose to respond kindly.

- **Choose to set a good example** – This is especially important if you have children of your own at home. The last kind of role model that you want to be is that of an angry parent. Do you want your kids growing up to become somebody who lashes out in anger all the time? Someone whom other people view as toxic individuals because they can't keep their temper under control? Children learn first and foremost by the example that you set for them, and if you are a parent who always gives into your angry desires, rants, shouts, raves, curses, and even hits family members in anger, this is what they will be observing. This is what they will grow up knowing, and without even realizing it, they'll be emulating your behavior. For the sake of your children, choose to set a good example. Lead by example and let the example be that there is always another way to resolve the conflict, which does not have to end in an angry argument. As a parent, you will be the one who sets the tone at home. What kind of tone do you want to set? One of harmony and love? Or one of anger?

- **Be open to conversation** – Don't be dismissive of another family member's concerns, unhappiness, or opinions. Don't be dismissive of conflicts because avoiding them is only going to make things much worse. Whenever there is a problem, you need to address it before it escalates and festers into an even bigger problem which may result in an angry shouting match between one, two, or several family members. What you are trying to do is learn how to catch and manage your anger at home before it can even hit, so if you see a concern or a possible conflict in the making, suggest that those involved sit down and have a heart-to-heart discussion about it. All conflicts can be resolved. We just have to make an effort to try. Be comfortable talking about what makes you angry. It is nothing to be ashamed of. Talking about it is much better than showing it.

- **Don't use anger as a form of punishment** – If you're guilty of giving family members the silent treatment for days or even weeks because you're angry, it is time to stop. That's not catching your anger; that's you giving in to your anger and choosing to wallow in it instead of finding constructive ways to resolve that anger. Ask yourself this, *What good is punishing them with my anger doing except creating disharmony and unhappiness in the family?* The answer will be nothing. Nothing good is going to come out of it. You're just going to cause many people to be unhappy and feel sad. It may give you a sense of satisfaction knowing you're inflicting this kind of emotional pain on others because you are feeling so angry, but it isn't worth it. These are people you love. What you should do is treat them with nothing but love and respect in return.

Catching Anger Before It Hits at Work

Anger at work could begin in the subtle form of a disgruntled employee. *You* could be that unhappy employee and the little things that start to aggravate you are slowly building up inside. You feel like you could be on the verge of exploding.

Some signs to look out for to identify if you or another employee is potentially feeling unhappy at work include:

- Losing interest in work.
- Becoming disagreeable. Everything is not right no matter what is said.
- Becoming antisocial by barely engaging with team members or other colleagues anymore.
- Becoming snappy when someone attempts to start a conversation.
- Appearing distracted and unfocused on work duties.
- Displaying a lack of respect for team members, maybe even superiors.
- Taking more sick days and finding excuses to stay away from work.
- No longer interested in giving 100% effort towards the company.
- Becoming vocal about dissatisfaction.

Do these signs sound relatable? Do you know someone within your workplace that might be he harboring some anger under the surface? Maybe you are feeling all these emotions, and you're just trying to keep your anger bottled in, but it's getting harder to control. The good news is you now know how to recognize these signs so that you can put a stop to it before your anger erupts at work. Maybe you could even offer to help out that disgruntled coworker so that *their* temper doesn't unleash.

To catch anger at work before it escalates into something unpleasant, here is what you need to do:

- **Learn to accept reality** – You may not be entirely happy with the way things are done in the company, but making major changes that better suit your needs is not your decision to make. Unless the company is yours of course. You always have a choice to leave and look for work elsewhere if being there is truly making you unhappy and irritable, but if you decide to stay, you need to accept the good and the bad about the job and face reality. If you notice your coworker feeling this way, offer to catch up over a chat and have a talk about it. Empathize with them. Tell them you understand how they feel because sometimes you feel the same way. Point out that there are options and it is up to them what they want to do. If you or your coworker decides to stay, then you need to learn to accept the reality that things are the way they are. They may change, or they may not, but there is no sense in getting all angry and worked up about it.

- **Don't take it personally** – The company's issues are not about you. You may not like the company's policy, but it isn't about you. You may not like the way certain things are done, but again it is not about you. The more you take things personally like there's a personal vendetta against you, the unhappier you are going to be. Some of your other coworkers may be just as unhappy about a policy or the way things are done, but they're not taking it personally and internalizing all that frustration until it becomes anger. Neither should you. It isn't about you; it's just business. Remember that if you don't like it, you always have a choice to seek employment elsewhere.

- **Take a step back** – Do you feel like you are working far too much and not being adequately rewarded for your efforts? The lack of recognition starts to aggravate you? Then take a step back and slow it down a little instead of getting all worked up about it. Simple, easy to resolve matters like these are just not worth wasting all your energy getting angry about. If your employer is not demanding that you work overtime for example, but you choose to do it anyway in the hopes of getting a big pay rise later, this was your decision to make. Nobody forced you into it, so don't be disgruntled and unhappy when you feel you are not being adequately rewarded. You always have a choice to take a step back and slow it down a little if it's getting to be too much.

- **Mingle with upbeat coworkers** – Not every employee is going to be as dissatisfied or unhappy with the company that they are working in. If you're working for a big organization, you will find lots of different personalities coming together under one roof. Seek out employees who have a positive outlook, who come to work with a smile on their face and a spring in their step, always looking forward to a brand-new day. Let their optimism rub off on you and help alleviate some of that pent-up frustration you've been feeling. Remember how in the earlier chapters we talked about keeping the right kind of company? This is something that you need to do at work too. Avoid colleagues who are just as unhappy and as miserable as you feel because getting together will only serve to fuel your feelings of dissatisfaction. What you're trying to do is put a stop to it before your anger can get the best of you at work, so you need to do the complete opposite and mingle with coworkers who can lift your spirits instead.

- **Look for the good in your job** – There must be at least one thing about your job that you're good at. Or something that makes you happy enough. Is it the flexible work hours? A good superior that you can talk to and who understands? Maybe the coworker in the next cubicle who never fails to make you laugh? Are you good at several aspects of your job which gives you a sense of accomplishment when you do it? Focus on the good things that you have to look forward to, instead of focusing on all the things which are making you grumpy and irritable at work. Make the positive aspects your primary focus. Each time that you feel yourself getting angry or feeling unhappy at work think about the good things about your job that you can look forward to each day. Think about it this way too: if your job really was that terrible, why are you still in it instead of looking for opportunities elsewhere?

Catching Anger Before It Hits at Public Arenas

In public we are, generally, on our best behavior because we are conscious of other people being around us. However, sometimes a moment of anger can strike, and you forget all about being out in public and just let your anger fly. It happens to the best of us. But all hope is not lost. There are still strategies and tools which you can use to help you catch your anger before it hits in public arenas.

- **Be more tolerant** – You are out and about in the world, and you have to share this world that we live in with millions of other people. Unlike your home, this is not a place where you can have things done your way. Or expect things to be done your way. It isn't about you when it comes to a public space; it is about everyone. If you choose to be intolerant and let the little things get to you, you're going to find it very challenging to keep your cool in public. You need to become a more tolerant person by accepting that you're not entitled to anything, and people are not here to conform to what you want. Just like how everyone else is tolerant about what you do in public, you need to show that same respect towards them. If you don't like something, there's always a choice to walk away and remove yourself from the situation.

- **Again, don't take it personally** – Just like at work, don't take it personally. Other people are just going about their business in public like you are. They are not there to purposely go out of their way to irritate or aggravate you. If you observe someone doing or saying something which starts to trigger your anger, remove yourself from the situation. You have a choice about it. You don't need to take it personally because this person is a complete stranger to you. Why should they purposely be doing something that annoys you?

- **Be polite and courteous** – The use of expletives these days happens all too frequently. It has become second nature to many of us to swear when things are not going our way. However, using an expletive in a public space could sometimes result in a case of saying something at the wrong time in the wrong place. This could then potentially lead to an argument because something you said angered someone else, who took it personally or misunderstood it. There are so many things which could go wrong in a situation like this, so if you want to do everything that you can to catch your anger and manage it within a public setting, you can start by doing the simple thing – be polite and courteous at all times whenever you're out in public.

- **Settle for being annoyed and walk away** – You don't have to allow yourself to reach a point of uncontrollable anger when you're out in public. Sometimes, certain circumstances may be unavoidable, and somehow, despite your best efforts, you find yourself in a situation that is causing (or going to cause you) a great deal of anger. How about a compromise instead? If you want to manage your anger better, learn to settle for just being annoyed or irritated and then immediately walk away or remove yourself from the situation. Don't stick around until your irritation escalates into something more. Being annoyed is also much easier to overcome and get over than anger. The next time that you find yourself in a situation that is inciting your anger try to keep things in perspective. Be annoyed but then make that the limit. There is no reason to take it any further. It is not the end of the world. Once again, don't take it personally. Settle for being annoyed and then walk away.

Chapter 8: Three Devils – The Relationship among Anger, Stress, and Anxiety

Anger, stress, and anxiety. Possibly the worst trifecta you could have. The three often run so closely together and the emotions become interchangeable that it is sometimes hard to tell where one ends and the other begins. Anger could be triggered by stress, stress could be triggered by anxiety, and anxiety could make way for anger which then leads to even more stress. Too much stress in your life could also cause anxiety and anger issues.

In this chapter, we will be exploring stress and anxiety in further detail and the link between those two emotions and how they could contribute to your anger issues.

Distinguishing Stress from the Rest

As the world continues to progress at a faster and faster pace, so do our stress levels because of our non-stop, hectic, and on the go lifestyles. Stress has become a normal part of our everyday living. The early humans also felt stress, but not in the same way that we do today. Their version of stress was what activated their fight or flight response when they had to survive in the wilderness. It helped them survive and stay alive. It helped them hunt, respond quickly when danger was present, and it is a very large part of why the human race is still going strong today.

When you think about the word stress, what image springs to mind? Or what do you associate with the term stress? Something that is bad for you? Something that wreaks havoc in your life and on your health? Something that causes you constant headaches? Stress has certainly got a bad reputation for itself because of the negative connotations associated with it.

As much as we would like it to be so, it's almost impossible to feel happy-go-lucky and carefree all the time. You can try your best to remain positive and optimistic each day, but there will be an occasion or several where you may feel stress knocking at your door. If only things could run smoothly all the time. That's where stress comes into play. There are two types of stress, and we ordinarily deal with one good and one bad.

Good stress can be beneficial and can even motivate you to perform better than you ordinarily would. The bad stress is the one that is associated with anxiety, possibly causing depression if it is experienced at a chronic level and a whole host of other health-related problems. The bad stress is the one that contributes and even triggers our anger.

What happens to your body when you typically feel stressed include:

- Pupil dilation
- Blood pressure levels rise
- Your heart rate increases
- Your breathing quickens
- Your muscles feel tense and tight especially around your shoulders
- Adrenaline starts pumping through your body which is why you often feel a sudden "surge" or "rush"
- You start sweating profusely, especially on your palms
- Your cortisol levels increase

There's a lot that can happen to your body when you're feeling stressed. No wonder it is such a draining emotion, just like anger is. As with your anger, stress can be caused by several factors, and it would help you to begin identifying what the cause of your stress is.

Some examples of stress triggers could include situations, circumstances, certain people, events, your job, deadlines, traffic, an emotional situation, relationships, heartbreak, death, starting a new phase in life, sudden change, and more. Stress can be caused by a wide variety of factors and differs between individuals. What is a stress trigger for one person may not be one for someone else.

Stress can be categorized into two types. One is major stress triggers, and the other is minor stress triggers. Some examples of major stress triggers include the following:

- Contracting a chronic illness
- Being fired from your job
- Being yelled at by your boss
- Financial matters

- Having big bills to pay each month
- Experiencing death
- Having a major life change happen

Some examples of minor stress triggers include:

- When you're rushing to meet a deadline
- When you're hurrying to meet a friend or an appointment, and you're at risk of running late
- Being disturbed when you're in the middle of something
- Heavy traffic and rush hour
- When someone has taken one of your things without permission and used it
- Looking after a sick family member
- Rushing from one task to the next
- When you've misplaced something important
- When someone is running late to an appointment you set up
- Meeting difficult clients

Each person would have a different tolerance for stress. Some people can handle large amounts of stress well and still maintain a cool head on their shoulders. Others, who don't cope with stress as well, end up tense, frustrated, and – you guessed it – angry. While bad stress in small doses is still manageable, there are certain types of stress which are bordering on toxic. The toxic stress is the one you want to stay away from because it does nothing to help try and manage your anger issues.

The toxic types of stress include the following:

- ***The type of stress that is cumulative***

This type of stress tends to accumulate over time (just like your anger does). When things pile on top of each other, your stress tends to grow and build like a snowball, until one day, it bursts forth either in the form of anger or anxiety. This usually happens when you reach a point where you can't take it anymore, and everything just feels like it is getting out of hand.

- ***The type of stress that is chronic***

This type of stress just always seems to hang around you and never fully goes away. It can be very toxic because it means you find yourself in a constant state of unhappiness, feel nervous or anxious, and always jumpy like you are just waiting for the next thing to go wrong in your life. It can also manifest itself as a chronic anger because you become snappy, irritable and you find it difficult to concentrate on any of the tasks that you're supposed to be doing.

Is this Anxiety? Or am I Just a Stressed-out Person?

Anxiety can sometimes be hard to distinguish from stress, especially if you don't know for sure that you may be dealing with anxiety in the first place. Ask yourself these questions for a moment:

- Do you find yourself feeling constantly tense and on edge all the time?

- Do your worries make you so fearful that it is all you can think about?

- Is what you are worried about starting to prevent you from running your daily routine normally because you're so worked up by it?

- Do those nagging thoughts just never seem to leave you?

If your worries are more than just temporary, sometimes bordering on fear, and they bother you more often than they should, you could be dealing with more than just stress. You could be dealing with anxiety.

Anxiety is a combination of several different factors which contribute to this emotion. It is the human body's natural response to stress. According to the American Psychological Association (APA), anxiety is an emotion which is characterized by feelings that include worried thoughts, tension, and even physical changes in the body, such as an increase in blood pressure. It is hard to pinpoint exactly what the causes of anxiety are because there are so many factors which could contribute towards a person experiencing anxiety. It is unique to each person, what they are going through, and what they may have experienced in the past.

Possible Causes of Anxiety

While it is hard to determine for sure what could cause someone to experience anxiety, there are several examples that we could look at for possible situations where a person's anxiety might be triggered. These situations include:

- **You fear rejection** – If you are someone who suffers from low self-esteem, having a fear of rejection is something which could potentially cause you to feel anxious. This is because you already have a low opinion of yourself. This low self- esteem is what is going to feed into your anxiety about being rejected by the people around you. The only thing you can think about is your flaws, and you can't comprehend why other people want to be around you in the first place. So you end up worrying and obsessing possibly every waking moment that one day you find yourself all alone with nobody to turn to, especially because of your issues with anxiety.

- **You fear to be alone** – Linked to the point above, a fear of being alone is also a possible cause for anxiety. Nobody ever really wants to be alone. Some people do enjoy the occasional solitude but being completely and utterly alone in this world is not something that anybody wants. Human beings are social creatures, and we crave intimacy and a connection with other human beings. Even the introverts. Dealing with anxiety, you constantly worry about being alone. You worry that your anxiety makes people turn away from you and they will not be able to love you for who you are because you've forgotten your own self-worth. You worry all the time, and one of your worst fears is that the people that love you will eventually give up on you because your anxiety becomes too much for them.

- **You fear change in your life** – Some people adapt and adjust well to the changes they experience in their life. Others, not so much. When major change takes place, it is normal to feel concerned about how everything is going to go, if things are going to work out for the best. If you are dealing with anxiety, this can be a trigger because anxiety causes you to be resistant to change. You're afraid of what is going to happen when things change, and you worry about whether you will be able to cope. What if you have a complete nervous breakdown? What is going to happen if you hate the new change that's taking place in your life? Anxiety can make it difficult for those who have it to be receptive to change, and they may take longer than usual to adapt and adjust to the new situations or surroundings that they are faced with.

How Do I Manage My Anxiety?

Nobody likes having anxious thoughts that disrupt their everyday routine. It's hard to function when all you can think about is your worries and what could go wrong at every turn. It is even worse when they become so bad that it causes you immense amounts of stress, which then leads to anger because the pressure just feels like it is too much to bear. Living with anxiety may not be easy, but at least there is something you can do about it.

The following strategies will help you manage and keep your anxiety in check, so you can then learn to manage your stress and anger much better.

- **Question yourself** – Or rather, your thoughts whenever they pop up and threaten to jumpstart your anxiety and make you stressed. Whenever you start having an anxious thought, stop and ask yourself why this is happening? What is the root cause of that worry and is it justifiable to worry this much about it? Look for your triggers and identify what is making you feel this way. Ask yourself if you are worrying for nothing. Or do you have tangible facts to go on? Take a moment to question your worry and work through whether this is something that you should get anxious over or not.

- **Identifying your triggers** – Just like the other two emotions, you need to apply that same process here. Everyone has different anxiety triggers, and it is important to learn what yours are. What is causing you to feel anxious right now? Is it something that you're dealing with at work or in your personal life? What about your relationships? Are you currently going through something stressful which causes anxious thoughts? Identifying your triggers will give you a better handle at controlling your anxiety because you will come to know what to expect and you'll be able to take the necessary pre-emptive measures to prepare for it.

- **Ensure that you're getting a good night's sleep** – It is often underestimated how important getting a good night sleep is. It is such a simple yet effective tool which unfortunately most people do not follow enough. Feeling anxious all the time can cause you to feel drained and fatigued, two emotions that stop you from performing or going through the day at your fullest potential. When you're in this state, you're unable to focus or think as clearly as you should. Situations and circumstances which are manageable somehow suddenly seem like an impossible task to overcome. Start making it a habit to always get a good night's sleep each night with the recommended number of hours, so you're always feeling your best. It'll help to keep your stress and anger under control too.

- **Keep a thought journal** – Now, before you dismiss this and say journaling or writing is not something for you, consider the benefits first. Often, our anxious thoughts and worries can seem magnified and worse than they should when they're bottled up inside our minds with no escape outlet. This is how it leads to stress and unchecked anger because we're not coping and dealing with it properly the way that we should. This is why keeping a thought journal is going to be so useful. Whenever you're feeling anxious or an anxious thought is nagging you, pour it all out onto your journal. Instead of unleashing all that pent-up emotion in the form of anger against someone else, isn't it better to let it out in your journal where no one gets hurt? Your journal is for you and you alone. Be free and pour your heart and soul into it. Nobody is going to judge you for it. Nobody will even see your innermost thoughts. It is a private space for you and you alone to process and work through everything that you're feeling.

- **Lean on those you can trust** – Don't be afraid to ask for help when something seems too overwhelming. Going through a challenge always feels more manageable when you've got someone you can trust to help you through it. It makes a world of difference when you're dealing with it on your own and when you have the proper support system in place. This could be all it takes to mean the difference between successfully managing your anxiety, stress and anger, and failure to do so. Find a circle of people – friends or family – that you trust completely to be there for you and lean on them for support.

- **Be patient with yourself** – If only getting rid of anxiety were that simple. We would all like to toss our anxieties out the window and get rid of them just like that. Unfortunately, it isn't quite as simple as that. Just like overcoming and learning how to manage your anger, there is no magic formula, no shortcut to the process, no overnight solution that is going to work miracles. Overcoming anxiety is a process which takes time, and you need to prepare yourself for that to avoid frustrations along the way. Start small by making little daily goals for yourself to help you overcome your anxious thoughts over time and eventually with each little success, your confidence will grow as you get better at taking control over your anxiety.

If despite using the methods above, you are still having a very difficult time coping and managing your anxiety, you would need to consider getting treatments to help you overcome these emotions. The following examples are instances of when you should consider getting a medical opinion for your anxiety issues:

- When you have reason to believe that an underlying medical condition is causing your anxiety.

- When your anxiety is causing you to have suicidal thoughts and a tendency to inflict self-harm.

- When you feel like your anxieties are too much to bear, and they are still out of control despite your best efforts at managing them.

- When going through and functioning each day becomes too difficult to do anymore.

- When you feel the urge to turn towards substances like drugs or alcohol to help you cope with your anxiety.

If at any point you are genuinely concerned about your health and wellbeing, you should seek the advice of a medical professional immediately. Anxiety could lead to other serious medical conditions if not treated properly and we're not talking about just anger and stress-related issues anymore.

Chapter 9: When it isn't you – How to Deal with Angry People

Sometimes it's you, and sometimes it isn't. There could be times when *your* anger is not the problem. It's not you; it's them. It seems like a lot, doesn't it? Having to manage your anger issues *and* learning how to deal with angry people on top of that.

How do you deal with angry people without running the risk of losing your temper and still resolving the situation in responding and reacting appropriately to reach an amicable resolution? Through communication.

In times of anger, there is a distinctive communication breakdown, especially when both people engaged in a confrontation are angry individuals who have lost control of their emotions. Communication is a complex matter as it is whether in everyday life or at work. When you're dealing with it in anger, it becomes even more complex. Misinterpretations can cause even more anger. Messages that don't come across clearly cause even more anger and frustration on both parts.

Some of the common communication barriers which are likely to occur when you're dealing with one or several angry individuals include the following:

- **Making assumptions** – This is a dangerous one when you're dealing with angry individuals. Making assumptions is a common communication barrier, and this frequently occurs when someone decides to reach a decision or course of action without fully listening to all the information at hand. Do you see why active listening is such an important skill to have when it comes to learning how to manage anger? Making assumptions can lead to complications because when you are not well informed, you run the risk of making more mistakes than you should. By assuming you know how the person is thinking, feeling, or what they mean by their actions, you run the risk of making the situation much worse.

- **Not giving your full attention** – Not giving your full attention to the person who is speaking to you is considered a communication barrier. If you were the angry party who was trying to convey your message and you noticed that the other person was not giving you their full attention, what do you think would happen? Chances are you'd probably get even angrier. Admittedly, yes, sometimes, our mind tends to wander or drift when someone else is talking. When attention starts to drift, it can be easy to miss crucial points in the message, and when you're dealing with an angry person, it is even more important than ever to pay attention to detail if you want to maintain any hopes of resolving the situation amicably.

- **Using expletives or jargon** – Using expletives is a definite *no* when it comes to trying to diffuse an angry situation. Even if you feel like you may be on the verge of not being able to hold back any longer, tap into your willpower a little bit more and just don't do it. Also, using jargons can be a communication barrier too in a situation like this. Not everyone may be familiar with certain jargons, and sometimes these unfamiliar terms can cause confusion and complicate things for the person who is trying to understand your message. In an angry situation, not being able to understand might cause even more frustration, irritation, and anger.

- **Saying too much at once** – In their anger, a person may be rushing through their message, trying to get everything out there in the open. Making it clear how angry they may be feeling. Or, in your attempt to try and calm the person down, you could be the one rushing through your message trying to make yourself heard. One thing that everyone would do well to remember when it comes to communication is that not everyone thinks, reacts, or processes information in the same way. One person may be able to process information quickly and efficiently, while someone else may need more time to digest that same piece of information properly. This can prove to be a hindrance when you're trying to deal with an angry individual because you could risk just aggravating them even more. If they feel frustrated at not being able to understand what you're saying, that will only serve to fuel their anger even more. Delivering too much too soon runs the risk of overwhelming the receiver, and as a result, they may not be able to fully process or understand what it is that you're trying to convey. Misunderstandings can often occur in this case, which may lead to – you guessed it – even more anger. In this scenario, it may be best just to let them do all the talking first before you speak up and say anything.

How to Deal with Angry People

To learn how to manage someone else's anger, so it doesn't rub off on you and threaten to derail your attempts at managing your anger, use the following guidelines to help you.

- **Focus on the problem at hand** – It can be hard to lose sight of what you should be focusing on when you're dealing with someone who is threatening to raise your anger to the surface, but it is important that you remain calm in this situation. Focus on dealing with the problem at hand and not the angry person that is in front of you. It is easy to feel like the angry person is personally attacking you, but if you get to the root of the problem, you'll find that is not always the case.

- **Be the cool cucumber in this case** – This can be a very difficult thing to do, admittedly, but *someone* has got to keep a cool head. Otherwise, the argument could get really ugly. That is the last thing that you want, where the two of you end up in a shouting match against one another, possibly saying things which can never be taken back. Tap into every ounce of willpower that you have to remain the one who stays calm in this situation. Remember that this person is going through the same thing that you are. You were once in a position where you had a lot of trouble learning how to control and manage your anger. Empathize and see things from their point of view. Be the bigger person that encourages them to remain calm and remind them to calm down and resolve the problem in a more civilized manner. Don't internalize their anger and make it your own; remember, it may not be about you at all. They're just having trouble properly channeling their anger in the right way.

- **Keep your tone polite and civil** – It can be very easy to fall into the trap of shouting back to defend yourself when someone is yelling at you. However, this, of course, is the last thing that you should do. What you should do instead is to keep your tone polite and civil throughout the conversation, regardless of the way that the other person is acting. When you're angry, the way that you say things and your tone of voice can incite just as much anger as the words that you say. When you keep your tone civil, there is a much higher chance that the other person will calm down and start to lower their tone of voice too when they see that you're not yelling back at them. It can be very humbling for the angry person, and it may just make them stop and think twice about the way they are acting.

- **Always be respectful** – Even if the other person is not. The way they behave is not your responsibility. You are responsible for your actions, and you should do everything that you can to ensure you don't do anything that you will only regret later on. Maintain respectful behavior throughout the conversation, and this will reflect on your maturity. It will also say a lot about how far you have come in terms of your anger management attempts. Under no circumstance during a confrontation with another angry individual should you roll your eyes, display sarcasm, make snide remarks that will only incite them further, point blame, lecture, criticize, or use foul language.

- **Ask for a timeout if you need it** – You have every right to ask for one if you feel the situation calls for it. Walk away and come back to the conversation later when you've got a much clearer head and the other person has had some time to calm down. This is especially important if you're finding it harder to control your levels of anger at this point, and instead of running the risk of letting your temper fly, take a timeout. Speak up and let the other person know that you feel this would be better discussed at a more appropriate time. If they disagree, be firm about it and request that they respect your decision.

- **Clarify and confirm** – Angry people want to be heard and understood. They want others to know why they are feeling the way that they are, what's upsetting them, and why they are so frustrated. To help diffuse the situation and come to an amicable agreement or solution, spend some time clarifying and ensuring that you understood what they were trying to say. Also, make sure that they understood what *you* are trying to say. To help you determine if your message is clear enough, ask yourself if the objective of the message is clear and if you are getting all the important information across. Let them know that you hear what they are saying and you're doing your best to try and help them solve the problem.

- **Using the right words** – This is just as important as watching the tone of your voice. Sometimes all it takes is for someone just to say one wrong thing to make a bad situation worse. Word selection is important in determining how effective your messages come across. Words are the source of facilitating effective communication, and careless or improper use of words are usually the reason for misplaced anger. In an attempt to try and effectively handle difficult individuals, think about using the right types of words when you're in a conversation with them. Opt for common and familiar words, single words which deliver the point across more concisely instead of several words. Use shorter words where possible. Speak succinctly and clearly. The more concise and succinct your message, the easier it is to understand, and the less chance there is for misunderstandings to occur.

- **Don't appear superior** – While you may be the bigger person in this situation and the one who is trying to keep the peace, avoid inflicting an air of superiority when dealing with an angry individual. You'll have a better chance of effectively dealing with them if you are relatable. Talk to them like an equal because this helps them be more receptive and attentive to the things you have to say, even when they are angry.

Learning How to Communicate Properly with Angry Individuals

Now that we have established the importance of communication when dealing with an angry individual, here comes the next question – how do you work on improving your communication skills so you can effectively deal with angry individuals? You have your own anger management issues to contend with, and that is already a lot to deal with. Dealing with other angry individuals may be aggravating to you because it makes it harder to keep a firm control of your temper. However, communicating with them well, making yourself understood *and understanding them* is essential if you hope to resolve an angry situation as peacefully as possible.

In a situation like this, both your verbal and non-verbal skills are going to come into play. It is not just about the way that you speak, but also the manner in which you carry yourself that makes you an effective communicator overall. For example, if you were to come off with an aggressive body stance, an angry expression on your face, and arms folded in front of your chest, what kind of message does that send to the other person? If they were already feeling angry, this would just make them even angrier because they perceive you as someone who is hostile right from the beginning, even before you have said a word. If you want to be successful, you are going to need to hone your skills in both of these areas.

When communicating with an angry individual (or several), here is what you need to do:

- **Think, hold and then speak** – To communicate effectively with angry people, you need to learn not to say the first thing that pops into your mind. Effective communicators, in general, are ones who think before they speak because they know that if they don't, they run the risk of saying the wrong thing or causing misunderstanding. It helps if you were to hold off on responding immediately when dealing with an angry individual. Quickly run through what you were about to say and make sure it is okay and then only speak. Do not give in to the urge to respond with the first thing that pops into your head. It is completely okay to pause for a moment, take a beat to really think about what you're going to say, and then speak.

- **Using the right body language** – Even though you may not have any friendly feelings towards the person who is currently displaying their anger towards you, you would still need to make a conscious effort to keep your body language as welcoming as possible. Adopt an open, welcoming, and inviting body language because it is one of the most important factors you need to bear in mind when you're dealing with someone who is angry. Go back to the earlier scenario about what happens if when you're angry, you had to deal with someone who was equally hostile and making their annoyance blatant. What we are not saying outright can reveal more about how we really feel and body language is far more revealing than your words will ever be. Our bodies are capable of communicating without ever saying a word so watch your body language when you are having a conversation, especially with someone who is already emotional and angry. Maintain good eye contact, avoid crossing your arms in front of your chest, smile, don't put your hands in your pockets, and adopt a relaxed posture and hold your head up high with confidence.

- **Avoid mumbling too much** – You need to be able to speak clearly and project your voice when dealing with angry people. But not in a way that makes it appear as though you're shouting back at them. Just speak clearly enough to be heard over their raised tone of voice. Avoid being meek, soft and mumbling or muttering your words because they won't be able to hear what you're saying. If they can't hear you properly in their angry state, they could assume you're muttering something rude or offensive about them under your breath. This will only make them even angrier because they are already in a heightened emotional state as it is. Speak clearly and project, but maintain a respectful tone of voice.

- **Speak with patience** – You basically have to be the complete opposite of what the angry individual is. They are the emotional one, and you now need to be the calm and patient one. Speak in soothing tones and keep reminding yourself that this is not personal. They just happen to be very emotional right now, and they're not thinking straight. It is easy to get impatient with someone when they are unleashing their anger towards you with what seems like no regard for your feelings or emotions. Demonstrating your patience in a moment like this is a reflection on you as a person and how far you have come at managing your issues with anger. The fact that you can exude patience in a moment like this is something you should definitely be proud of because this is the ultimate demonstration of self-control.

The skills that you learned in this chapter will not only help you effectively manage the angry people that you have to deal with, but it will also give you some perspective into what other people have to put up with each time you fail to manage your anger. Use moments like this as a time for some internal reflection, to think about how this is what other people have to put up with whenever you're angry and treating them the same way. This can be one of those moments of clarity, where it dawns on you just how important it is to learn how to manage your anger because you don't want to continue treating other people this way. Use this as a great learning opportunity – because it is.

Chapter 10: Tricks and Tips – How to Handle Road Rage, Intimacy, and Other Specific Anger Issues

Having as many strategies, tips, and tricks for success can go a long way in helping you learn how to manage your anger much better, especially during specific moments like road rage, where it seems much harder to control yourself behind the wheel of your car. Or maybe you're in need of some advice about how to not let anger affect moments of intimacy.

Anger can be managed. It can be controlled, and it doesn't have to be a destructive force in your life. You have it within you to make these positive changes in your life for the better. With the additional tricks and tips that you will read about in this chapter, anger management is even easier than ever.

General Tips to Better Manage Your Anger

- **Have your own space** – Whether you're living alone or with someone, it helps to have a little space of your own at the end of the day where you can just spend a couple of minutes alone unwinding. Maybe create a little comfort zone of your own at home that helps promote feelings of calm and a sense of contentment. Turn a corner of your favorite room in your home into a special area where you can find your Zen and calm. Make this a space that you look forward to coming home to every day. This room should be free from distraction, makes you feel comfortable, and most importantly, it has to be somewhere that you want to be. Remove anything that can be a distraction, disconnect your phone, and shut yourself off from the world for just a few minutes each day where you can come and find and connect with yourself once more. It is a great way to center yourself and unwind after what may have been a long, tiring, and hectic day.

- **Exercise, make it a habit** – It cannot be stressed enough just how beneficial exercise can be for you. If you're not already working out regularly, start doing it. It is an excellent stress relief outlet, and you will feel better about yourself in a way you haven't before. It elevates your mood, keeps you fit and healthy, and more importantly, it is a way for you to let go of the pent-up emotions you've been carrying around all day. Just 30 minutes a day is all you need. Run it out. Kickbox it out. Dance it out. Do yoga if it helps you to relax. Exercise is one of the best remedies you can get your hands on when it comes to learning how to manage your anger, and if you're not already doing it, start now!

- **Start the day the right way** – Establishing a morning routine is one way to approach this. Having a great morning routine that leaves you charged up and energized is a great way to start every day on a positive, motivated note. If you've been waking up in a bad mood for far too long now, only thinking about the stress and everything you need to deal with for the day, it's time to change that. Why should you start developing a better morning routine for yourself? Because a morning routine or habit will help you focus your mind at the start of every day. It is a habit that successful people abide by, which would explain how they manage to stay optimistic, even in the face of great challenge. Incorporate a morning routine into your lifestyle that is going to help you clear your mind, stay focused, stay optimistic, and mentally prepare you for the rest of the day ahead.

- **Choose an activity a day which inspires you** – When was the last time you did something that inspired you to make a change for the better? That reawakened that motivation within you to want to do something to improve your life? If you can't even remember the last time you felt that way, you've been angry for far too long. What you need to do right now is start choosing activities which are going to inspire you. Doing this daily would be great, but if you can't manage that, several times a week would work too. Watch a Ted Talk, listen to inspirational podcasts, read biographies of successful people, or any inspirational books you can get your hands on. You'll find there are plenty of opportunities for you to do this during the day. For example, while you're on your lunch break, commuting to work, while you get ready in the morning or before going to bed at night. You could even do it while you take your short coffee breaks at work. There are plenty of opportunities all around you just waiting to be seized. All you need to do is start noticing them. And it only takes a few minutes to listen to something inspirational every day to keep you motivated doing what you love.

Having a morning routine or habit will help you focus your mind at the start of every day. Many notably successful people like Tony Robbins have been known to incorporate a morning routine into their lifestyle to help them clear their minds, stay focused, and mentally prepare for anything they need to do that day.

Tips to Help You Deal with Road Rage

Road rage is one of the most common reasons for getting angry while we're driving on the road. If this rings all too true to you, don't worry. Here are some effective strategies that you could use to help you stay much calmer on the road.

- **Avoid rushing** – Managing your time and being more organized can go a long way towards making a difference. Road rage is often triggered when you're in a hurry to get somewhere, and everything on the road seems to be delaying you. You get stressed, worked up, and increasingly frustrated as you realize you're closer to missing your appointment or running late to where you need to be. If you know there is somewhere you need to be, leave earlier than you initially planned to give yourself plenty of time to get there and minimize the reasons for the delay. For example, if you planned to leave by 10:00 am, adjust your schedule so that you leave at 9:30 am instead or earlier if you'd like. When you're not rushing, anxious, and pressed for time, it minimizes the aggravation that you feel when you are behind the wheel.

- **Relax in your car** – Are you tense each time you get behind the wheel? The next time you hop into your car, be mindful about how you're feeling. Do your shoulders feel tense? Are you gripping the wheel far too hard because you're feeling stressed? Taking some measures to relax before you even begin your drive can put you in a much calmer state. Maybe play your favorite relaxing tunes, or take a couple of deep, measured breaths as you adjust and get comfortable in the car. Smile and say today is going to be a great day as you buckle in. Relaxing or even playing a podcast that puts you in good spirits is a great way to set the tone for a good drive ahead.

- **Be considerate** – Being polite and courteous is not just an anger management method that is reserved only for when people are in front of you. This concept can even be applied when you're driving on the road. The road is a space for everyone; we all need to share. Nobody is entitled to anything. We all need to make an effort to be respectful of others on the road. Be polite and courteous even when you're driving. Give way to others instead of rushing to block them off and stop them from cutting in front of you. It never hurts to be politer. If other drivers are not, you don't have to be like them. Put yourself in the other driver's shoes. Maybe they are in a hurry to get somewhere for reasons of their own. If you were in a hurry, wouldn't you appreciate it each time someone gave you way without getting angry with you? Kindness can begin with you.

- **Avoid driving if you're in a bad mood** – There will be moments where you already leave your home in a bad mood because something happened. Beginning a drive in a bad mood is only going to aggravate your road rage tendencies. Instead, you should avoid driving altogether if you know that you're not exactly feeling your best. Maybe take an Uber that day and let someone else do the driving so you can make an effort to calm down in the back seat and put yourself in a better mood. Doesn't that sound like a better option? And it keeps your road rage tendencies at bay.

Keeping Anger Out of Your Relationships – Tips to Rebuild that Spark and Reconnect on an Intimate Level Again

Anger can put a great deal of strain on a relationship. It is not easy being around someone who frequently loses their temper, and even though they may apologize later for it, the emotional damage has already been done with the words that have been said. The actions that you do in anger, just like your words, can never be undone. This is what your partner is going through each time you're unable to manage your anger appropriately. Just because they love you, it doesn't make it any easier to put up with this part of your personality.

Which is why the best thing you can do for your relationship is to learn how to manage that anger. To bring the love, spark, and intimacy back into the relationship. To breathe life into it once more. The following tips will help you with this part of the process:

- **Talk to your partner** – This is the first step in the process. Talk to your partner, sit down, and have a real heart-to-heart with them. Let them know that you realize there is a problem and that you're doing everything you can to manage your anger better. Let them know how much you appreciate their love and support as you work on becoming better. Emphasize how appreciative you are for everything that they have done for you and that you're sincerely sorry for everything they have to put up with whenever you lose your temper. Having a deep, meaningful conversation will let your partner know what's happening and ensure that the two of you are on the same page. This makes it easier to lean on your partner for support in the moments that you need them.

- **Start spending time as a couple again** – It's easy to get caught up with your own schedules. There always never seems to be enough time to get everything done in a day. However, you need to *make* the time if you want to fix your relationship – do things that are fun, and have fun together, enjoying each other's company, especially if you've got a lot of work to do in rebuilding a relationship that has been damaged by anger. When you're having fun together and enjoying activities that bring you closer to each other, it helps to strengthen the bond that you have. It may even remind the two of you about what you loved most about each other in the first place (something which can easily be forgotten when too much anger has been thrown into the mix). For it to work effectively, pick activities that both of you enjoy doing together as a couple, not just an activity that one person is going to enjoy. Both of you need to equally have fun because that is how you bond and you're going to need to do a lot of bonding and healing to recover from the strain that anger has caused.

- **Keep reminding your partner how much you love and appreciate them** – It is easy for your partner to feel taken for granted if all they're getting is bursts of anger and temper tantrums from you. It can be easy to feel unloved when someone is always snapping at you. It's easy to question why you're in this relationship and putting up with all your partner's temper tantrums. These are all the perspectives you need to consider regarding what your partner may be going through each time you lose your temper and let anger take control, damaging the relationship. Which is why now, as part of your anger management exercise, you need to make it a point to constantly remind your partner how much you love and appreciate them at every opportunity you get.

Thoughts to Free Yourself from Anger

When we feel angry, we tend to forget that we always have a choice. Anger binds us into this narrow, tunnel vision way of thinking and looking at the world, which is why it is often so hard to overcome anger when it hits. To free yourself from anger and learn how to manage it better, you need to realize that:

- **Anger and people do not have power over you** – Nobody has power over you, not even your emotions. Nobody has the power to make you angry unless you *allow* them to make you angry. Your emotion does not have the power to get the best of you unless you *allow* it to. All the power sits with you, and when you realize that, you'll see how much easier it becomes to manage your anger, and the next time you find yourself in a situation which could potentially trigger your anger again, tell yourself, *Nope, I will not allow this to have the power to make me angry and walk away.*

- **What goes around comes around** – What you put out there in the world comes back to you. It may sound like just another clichéd saying, but it has truth to it. If you go about constantly angry, bitter, and upset all the time, ready to bite the head off the next person who annoys you, that is all you are going to see mirrored back at you. People won't be nice. People won't be kind. People won't be understanding. People appear grumpy, annoyed, and angry around you too. Why? Because this is what you're putting out there in the world. Try the opposite this time and put a little love and happiness out there instead, and see what gets reflected back at you.

- **People are not your enemies** – Nobody is going out of their way to make you angry on purpose. Nobody wants to go around purposely provoking others to anger. Sometimes, situations and circumstances just can't be helped, despite your best efforts. The sooner you realize that people are not your enemy, that they're not purposely setting out with the intention to raise your anger, the better it will be for you when it comes to keeping your anger under control. Learn to see people, even complete strangers, as your allies and friends. You never know where new connections could lead, what new opportunities could form from the relationships that you make.

Conclusion

Thank you for making it through to the end of this book. It should have been informative and provided you with all of the tools you need to achieve your goals, whatever they may be.

As you've seen, anger, when misdirected, can often result in great unhappiness for both you and the people around you. Poorly managed anger can be a source of great pain, but now you know that it doesn't have to be this way. Not in the least.

You have the power within you to learn how to channel your anger, control it, and manage it in far more positive ways, which will lead to more desirable, happier outcomes. When channeled correctly, your anger can be a source of great good which pushes you to accomplish your goals.

It is also important to remember to take the time to stop and appreciate just how far you have come with your efforts to manage your anger. Picking up this book and working with the strategies in it is already a major step in the right direction, and you should be proud that you're making the change to become a better, healthier version of yourself. You and the people around you will certainly appreciate how hard you're working towards keeping your anger under control.

With the strategies you are now equipped with, you will be well on your way to better anger management as long as you persevere and persist even in the challenging moments. One great tip to know for sure that things are changing for the better: you'll know you've made momentous strides when all the things that used to set off your anger before no longer bother you as much.

The journey to gaining control over your anger will be a journey that keeps on going, something that is always a work in progress. However, each day, you get better and each day is a new opportunity for you to grow stronger and gain an even firmer grasp on the emotion that once left you out of control. Take each day in stride as there is always something new to be learned, and most importantly, enjoy the journey because you're becoming a better version of yourself each day.

Finally, if you found this book useful in any way, a review on Amazon is always appreciated!

EMPATH

Your Guide to Understanding Empaths and Their Emotional Abilities to Feel Empathy, Including Tips for Highly Sensitive People, Dealing with Energy Vampires, and Being a Psychic Empath

Steven Turner

DARK PSYCHOLOGY

What Machiavellian People of Power Know about Persuasion, Mind Control, Manipulation, Negotiation, Deception, Human Behavior, and Psychological Warfare that You Don't

Steven Turner

DIALECTICAL BEHAVIOR THERAPY

THE ULTIMATE GUIDE TO USING DBT FOR BORDERLINE PERSONALITY DISORDER, DIFFICULT EMOTIONS AND MOOD SWINGS, INCLUDING TECHNIQUES SUCH AS MINDFULNESS AND EMOTION REGULATION

STEVEN TURNER

Manufactured by Amazon.ca
Bolton, ON

25813647R00088